T0247875

Is There Extraterrestrial Life?

The Editors of *Scientific American*

SCIENTIFIC | EDUCATIONAL
AMERICAN | PUBLISHING

New York

Published in 2025 by Scientific American Educational Publishing
in association with **The Rosen Publishing Group**
2544 Clinton Street, Buffalo NY 14224

Contains material from Scientific American®, a division of Springer Nature America, Inc.,
reprinted by permission, as well as original material from The Rosen Publishing Group®.

First Edition

Scientific American
Lisa Pallatroni: Project Editor

Rosen Publishing
Danielle Haynes: Compiling Editor
Michael Moy: Senior Graphic Designer

Cataloging-in-Publication Data
Names: Scientific American Editors (New York, New York), editor.
Title: Is there extraterrestrial life? / The Editors of Scientific American.
Other titles: Scientific American explores big ideas.
Description: First edition. | New York : Scientific American Educational
Publishing, 2025. | Series: Scientific American explores big ideas |
Includes bibliographical references and index. | Audience: Grades 10-12 | Identifiers: LCCN
2024015427 | ISBN 9781725351875 (library binding) |
ISBN 9781725351868 (paperback) | ISBN 9781725351882 (ebook)
Subjects: LCSH: Life on other planets.
Classification: LCC QB54 .I78 2025 | DDC 576.8/39–dc23/eng/20240507
LC record available at https://lccn.loc.gov/2024015427

Manufactured in the United States of America
Websites listed were live at the time of publication.

Cover: diversepixel/Shutterstock.com

CPSIA Compliance Information: Batch # CSSA25.
For Further Information contact Rosen Publishing at 1-800-237-9932.

CONTENTS

INTRODUCTION

Have you ever looked up in the sky and wondered what's out there amongst the stars and all that seemingly infinite space? Or maybe you questioned whether humanity is really alone in this great big universe. This is something humans have been doing for as long as we've had records of life on Earth. Early humans kept track of time by drawing constellations on cave walls. These same stars have played important roles in various religions, including Christianity, Hinduism, and Judaism, as well as many Indigenous cultures.

Today, though, instead of drawing connections to the cosmos through spirituality and storytelling, humans investigate the sky using scientific theories and advanced technology. And one of the most important questions they seek to answer is whether there's life beyond this blue orb we call home. Better yet, have extraterrestrials already visited us?

The articles in this book will shed light on some of the current efforts to answer these questions as well as consider whether scientists are even taking the best approach. Section 1, "Searching Our Solar System," takes a look at exploration within our solar system, including investigations of Mars and Saturn. Section 2, "An Eye on UFOs," stays a little closer to home, questioning whether those mysterious lights in the night sky can be explained by extraterrestrials. Scientists mull the best way to interact with any potential alien species in Section 3, "Communicating with Aliens." Section 4, "Technology and the Search for Life," explores some of the newer tools and calculations scientists are using in their search for life. And finally, Section 5, "A New Approach," questions whether humans are going about the search for life in the best way possible. Maybe it's time to take a different view when looking out into the cosmos.

Section 1: Searching Our Solar System

New Evidence Discovered That Saturn's Moon Could Support Life

By Ling Xin

Saturn's ocean-covered moon Enceladus constantly spews water into space through fractures in its icy crust. The spacecraft *Cassini* determined the composition of these jets in the mid-2000s and found molecules that included carbon dioxide and ammonia, both crucial for life on Earth. And now, in a study published on Thursday in *Nature Astronomy*, scientists have reanalyzed the *Cassini* samples and revealed Enceladus's great chemical diversity—making this small icy moon the top candidate for finding alien life in our own solar system.

The study's lead author, Harvard University biophysicist Jonah Peter, was intrigued by previous findings that Enceladus was likely rich in organic compounds, most of which had not been identified. To figure out the moon's true chemical makeup, Peter and his colleagues at NASA's Jet Propulsion Laboratory reexamined data collected in 2011 and 2012 by the agency's Cassini-Huygens mission, which flew a spacecraft through Enceladus's spectacular water plumes multiple times. *Cassini*'s samples, analyzed by the spacecraft's onboard mass spectrometer (an instrument that identifies compounds by their molecular weight), had initially revealed five types of molecules in the jets: water, carbon dioxide, methane, ammonia, and molecular hydrogen.

For the new analysis, Peter and his colleagues took Cassini's data even further: they used a statistical analysis technique to compare the jet samples' molecular signatures with those of billions of potential combinations of known compounds. This allowed them to determine the plume's most likely components.

"Searching for compounds in the plume is a bit like putting the pieces of a puzzle back together," Peter says. "We look for the right combination of molecules that reproduce the observed data."

The team concluded that the icy jets included the five already identified molecules—but also some bigger, heavier compounds, including hydrocarbons such as hydrogen cyanide and ethane, as well as traces of partially oxidized compounds such as methanol.

The new results relied on a "smart and robust" statistical method to reveal these larger molecules, says Michel Blanc, a planetary scientist at the Research Institute in Astrophysics and Planetology in Toulouse, France, who worked on the Cassini mission. These compounds didn't show up in the initial analysis because the onboard instruments weren't equipped to identify them, he says. "Nobody in the Cassini-Huygens team had imagined that the small moons of Saturn could be chemically active and generate heavy molecules: that was, without doubt, the greatest surprise and likely the most important discovery of *Cassini*," Blanc adds.

Together with previously detected components such as water and ammonia, these newly discovered molecules could serve as building blocks and fuel for microbes, and they could potentially support an independent origin of life. Since the discovery of Enceladus's oceans, this moon has been a "prime target" in the search for the fundamental building blocks of life, Peter says.

Peter was especially excited to detect the presence of hydrogen cyanide, or HCN, because it is "one of the most important and versatile building blocks of life," he says. When combined with other molecules, HCN can help form nucleobases and amino acids, the precursors to more complex biochemistry such as proteins and RNA. Lab simulations have shown that these transformations are possible in environments that are similar to Enceladus's ice shell, Peter notes. "Many molecules important for the origin of life could have formed at Enceladus and could still be forming at Enceladus today," he says.

The plumes' diverse chemical composition points to high potential for oxidation-reduction, or "redox," reactions, which are often regarded as a key element in the synthesis of the building blocks of life—and in the biochemical processes that allow living organisms to breathe oxygen and photosynthesize.

The *Cassini* samples have now revealed the presence of both oxidized and reduced compounds in Enceladus's plumes. This is a "very exciting" result, says Kate Craft, a planetary scientist at the Johns Hopkins University Applied Physics Laboratory, who was not involved in the new study. These molecules could mix together, potentially through hydrothermal activity on the moon's seafloor, and could theoretically create "a habitable environment where life can be supported or might originate," Craft adds.

Scientists have no evidence to indicate such a process has actually occurred. In fact, it's not clear if or where these oxidized and reduced compounds might be meeting. And Craft points out that researchers still don't know exactly how the erupting water makes its way through the moon's ice shell.

Still, the findings may inform ongoing and planned missions to ocean worlds that are similar to Enceladus—including Jupiter's watery moon Europa, which likely has many of the same properties, Craft says. These questions will be further explored by the European Space Agency's *Jupiter Icy Moons Explorer* (*JUICE*) spacecraft, which is currently on its way to the Jupiter system.

The new findings also build a strong case for revisiting Enceladus in future space missions, Blanc says. Now that researchers know of the moon's stunning molecular diversity, they could use a mass spectrometer that is capable of studying bigger molecules to examine its complex chemical environment—and perhaps reveal the true habitability of this explosive moon.

About the Author

Ling Xin writes about physics, astronomy, spaceflight and related fields. More of her work can be found at lingxinwrites.com. Originally from Beijing, she is now based in Ohio.

Life on Mars May Have Been Its Own Worst Enemy

By Allison Gasparini

Although we know early Mars was wetter, warmer, and more habitable than today's freeze-dried desert world, researchers have yet to find direct proof that life ever graced its surface. If Mars did once host life, key questions remain: How did such life impact the planet, and where could we find evidence for its past existence? A new study considering these mysteries finds that a plausible Martian biosphere could have been instrumental for tipping the planet into its current inhospitable state. The findings further identify certain regions of Mars—including Jezero Crater, where NASA's *Perseverance* rover now roams—as most likely to host signs of this past life. And they ominously hint that life may be its own worst enemy on worlds throughout the cosmos.

Re-creating Mars as it was four billion years ago using climate and terrain models, researchers concluded methane-producing microbes could once have thrived mere centimeters below much of the Red Planet's surface, gobbling atmospheric hydrogen and carbon dioxide while protected by overlying sediment. But that buried biosphere would have ultimately retreated deeper into the planet, driven by freezing temperatures of its own making—perhaps to its doom.

Their study, published in *Nature Astronomy*, proposes that the interchange among hydrogen, carbon dioxide, and methane (all heat-trapping greenhouse gases) would have triggered global cooling that covered most of Mars's surface with inhospitable ice.

"Basically what we say is that life, when it appears on the planet and in the right condition, might be self-destructive," says study lead author Boris Sauterey, a postdoctoral fellow at Sorbonne University. "It's that self-destructive tendency which might be limiting the ability of life to emerge widely in the universe."

Gaia's Blessing—Or Medea's Curse?

In 1965 the late chemist and ecologist James Lovelock—then a researcher at NASA's Jet Propulsion Laboratory—argued that certain chemical compounds in an atmosphere act as biosignatures indicating life's presence on another world. On Earth, for instance, the coexistence of methane (from methane-producing bacteria, called methanogens) with oxygen (from photosynthetic organisms) constitutes a potent biosignature: each gas eradicates the other in ambient conditions, so the persistence of both indicates a steady replenishment most easily explained by biological sources.

Lovelock's work forms the basis of today's scientific search for alien life. It also informs the Gaia hypothesis, which he codified with biologist Lynn Margulis during the 1970s. This hypothesis, named after a "Mother Earth" deity from Greek mythology, suggests that life is self-regulating: Earth's organisms collectively interact with their surroundings in a way that maintains environmental habitability. For instance, higher global temperatures from excess atmospheric carbon dioxide also boost plant growth, which in turn siphons more of the greenhouse gas from the air, eventually returning the planet to a cooler state.

In 2009 University of Washington paleontologist Peter Ward put forward a less optimistic view. At planetary scales, Ward argued, life is more self-destructive than self-regulating and eventually wipes itself out. In contrast to the Gaia hypothesis, he named his idea after another figure from Greek mythology: Medea, a mother who kills her own children. To support his "Medea hypothesis," Ward cited several past mass extinction events on Earth that suggest life has an inherently self-destructive nature. During the Great Oxidation Event more than two billion years ago, for instance, photosynthetic cyanobacteria pumped huge amounts of the gas into Earth's oxygen-starved atmosphere. This eradicated the earlier dominant life-forms: methanogens and other anaerobic organisms for which oxygen was toxic. "You just look back at Earth's history, and you see periods where life was its own worst enemy," says Ward, who was not involved in the new study. "And I think this certainly could've been the case on Mars."

On Earth, though, the flood of oxygen also proved crucial for biological diversification and the eventual emergence of our biosphere's multicellular ancestors—showing that defining a situation as Gaian or Medean might be a matter of perspective. Until life is found on other worlds, however, we are left to examine the question through theoretical studies such as Sauterey's.

A Deeper Look for Martian Life

Kaveh Pahlevan, a research scientist at the SETI Institute, who was not involved in the study, says that the work "does broaden the way we think about the effects that biospheres can have on habitability." But he notes that it considers only the planet-altering effects of one metabolism type. The study would not capture the intricacy of something akin to the Great Oxidation Event, which hinged on the conflicting influences of methanogens and cyanobacteria. Sauterey acknowledges this limitation: "You can imagine that a more complex, more diversified [Martian] biosphere would not have had the negative effect on planet habitability that just methanogens would have had," he says.

The study highlights how a complex ecosystem, like that of early Earth, may be essential to recovery from otherwise catastrophic environmental change. And in Ward's view, an ascent toward ever greater complexity might help a biosphere avoid an otherwise-dismal Medean fate. "I truly believe the only way out—the only way any planet escapes once it gets life—is to evolve intelligence," he says. Only then, Ward says, could inhabitants develop solutions to mitigate Medean tendencies for life to foul its planetary nest.

The study did not consider the possibility of present-day methanogens lurking within the Martian subsurface. Such a situation could help explain enigmatic plumes of methane that scientists have repeatedly detected in the planet's atmosphere, although lifeless geophysical activity could also account for the plumes as well.

For ancient Mars, however, the study pinpoints places untouched by ice for large swaths of the planet's history—despite a near-global glaciation from a worldwide cooling event—where such microbes could have once thrived closer to the surface. One spot is Jezero Crater, the current target of the *Perseverance* rover's search for biosignature-bearing materials. But it is possible that fossil evidence of early methanogens would be under too much sediment for the rover to reach.

The study also identified two even more promising sites: Mars's Hellas Planitia and Isidis Planitia regions. These targets fit with a broader rising interest in examining the Martian subsurface for signs of life, says California Institute of Technology geobiologist Victoria Orphan, who was not involved in the study. Sauterey's research, Orphan says, is "a reference point to help stimulate debates and deeper thinking about future missions."

Sauterey is careful to point out that the new work is hypothetical—and that just because parts of Mars's crust were once habitable does not mean the planet was ever inhabited. Whether or not ancient methanogens ever lived on Mars, however, the results of the study illustrate how life itself can set the conditions for its own flourishing—or fizzling—on any world in the cosmos. Even single-celled organisms have the power to transform an otherwise habitable planet into a hostile place. And, Sauterey darkly adds, "with the technological means that we have, humans can do that even faster."

About the Author

Allison Gasparini is a science writer who has written for Forbes, Science News, *NASA, Brookhaven National Laboratory, the American Institute of Physics, Stanford University, and more. Follow her on X (formerly Twitter) @astrogasparini.*

At Jupiter, *JUICE* and *Clipper* Will Work Together in Hunt for Life

By Jonathan O'Callaghan

I f there is life elsewhere in our solar system, Jupiter's large icy moons are a pretty good bet on where to find it.

Scientists believe vast oceans lurk within them, kept liquid by the jostling from Jupiter's immense gravitational field and protected from the planet's harsh radiation belts by thick ice sheets. "What we've learned on Earth is where you find water, you quite often find life," says Mark Fox-Powell of the Open University in England. "When we look out in the solar system, places that have [liquid] water in the present day are really restricted to Earth and the moons of Jupiter and Saturn." That last planet and its satellites, studied in detail by NASA and the European Space Agency's Cassini-Huygens mission from 2004 to 2017, still hold secrets that scientists will one day probe. For now all eyes are on Jupiter.

A new mission to visit our solar system's largest planet and investigate the habitability of its moons is now set to begin. ESA's *JUICE*—the *Jupiter Icy Moons Explorer*—was shipped to French Guiana in South America for its April launch on a European Ariane 5 rocket. The six-ton *JUICE* spacecraft will take eight years to reach Jupiter, saving fuel along the way by using gravitational assists from Earth, Venus, and Mars. On its arrival in July 2031 the solar-powered machine will focus its 10 science instruments on three of the four largest Jovian moons—Europa, Ganymede, and Callisto—all thought to harbor subsurface oceans. Ganymede, the solar system's largest moon, will receive most of *JUICE*'s attention. After its initial reconnaissance, the spacecraft will enter orbit there in 2034. "We're trying to characterize what the habitability of Ganymede might be," says Emma Bunce of the University of Leicester in England, part of the *JUICE* team.

ESA isn't the only space agency with Jupiter in its sights. The concept that would ultimately become *JUICE* emerged in 2008 as part of the Europa Jupiter System Mission (EJSM), a joint venture with NASA. This collaborative effort called for Europe to build a Ganymede-focused spacecraft, while NASA would construct a probe for Europa. Funding issues in the U.S., however, led NASA to pull the plug on EJSM in the early 2010s, leaving Europe flying solo. "We didn't have the money," says Louise Prockter of the Johns Hopkins University Applied Physics Laboratory, part of the U.S. proposal team. "That killed the Europa part." The situation was disappointing but not wholly unexpected. "These things happen," says Michele Dougherty of Imperial College London, who worked on the European side of EJSM.

Redemption came in 2013, when NASA's efforts to explore Europa received renewed support and funding from Congress. Initially named the Europa Multiple Flyby Mission, the U.S. project eventually became Europa Clipper, after the "clipper" merchant ships of the 19th century. The international collaboration was reborn, mostly. "It's much reduced," Prockter says, although she estimates about 70 percent of the originally planned joint science will still be possible. With these two missions, our knowledge of Jupiter and its moons is set to increase substantially. The spacecraft will tell us whether life could exist in some of these worlds' bewildering subsurface oceans, laying the groundwork for later missions to look directly for evidence of such life, possibly even by diving into the oceans themselves. We can't yet travel to alien worlds around other stars, but Jupiter might offer the next best thing.

The First Moons

The jovian arena is often regarded as a miniature solar system because of the complexity and variety of the planet's moons—particularly its four largest, the Galilean moons, named for Italian astronomer Galileo Galilei, who discovered them in 1610. Their identification shook people's understanding of the universe, revealing the first known objects orbiting a body that was not the sun or Earth and thereby validating the Copernican model of the cosmos, which did not have us at its center. Jupiter is now known to have 92 natural satellites. Yet even Galileo might not have appreciated how fascinating his moons would turn out to be 400 years later or how pivotal they might prove in the hunt for life elsewhere in the universe.

The first spacecraft to venture into Jupiter's realm, moons and all, was NASA's *Pioneer 10* spacecraft. It flew past the planet in December 1973, providing our first close-up images of the magnificent gas giant. The flyby of NASA's *Voyager 1* spacecraft in March 1979 proved even more remarkable. The spacecraft's images of the moon Europa revealed that it had a bright, icy surface devoid of craters, hinting that some kind of resurfacing process was keeping its crust fresh and unblemished. The best bet was an unseen reservoir of liquid water below the surface, scientists surmised—an enticing option given that on Earth, life follows water.

In December 1995 NASA's Galileo mission became the first to orbit Jupiter, making numerous discoveries—for example, that the planet's third-largest moon, Io, is the most volcanically active world in the solar system. Data that Galileo took at Europa in 1996 found that something was disrupting Jupiter's magnetic field, offering stronger hints of a liquid sloshing under Europa's surface. The best evidence for a liquid ocean on Europa came two decades later, when the Hubble Space Telescope spotted plumes of water escaping from the moon's surface. The *Galileo* spacecraft orbited Jupiter for eight years, ending in 2003, and was "a fantastic mission," says Olivier Witasse of ESA, the project scientist for *JUICE*. "We are really going on the shoulders of Galileo."

No other probe would orbit Jupiter until the arrival of NASA's *Juno* spacecraft in 2016. Juno is still operational today, but it is focused on Jupiter itself, swinging past it in a looping orbit to probe the planet's interior, image its violent storms and monitor its immense magnetic field. The spacecraft has taken some images of Jupiter's moons, but it'll take dedicated missions to really expose their secrets. And that's where *JUICE* and *Clipper* come in.

Moon Hopping and Plume Spotting

Clipper will launch in fall 2024 on a SpaceX Falcon Heavy rocket. Despite its later launch date, its more powerful launch vehicle will allow the spacecraft to reach Jupiter more than a year before *JUICE*, in April 2030. It will not orbit Europa like *JUICE* will Ganymede, because Europa's proximity to Jupiter places it perilously deep within the planet's radiation belts. Instead *Clipper* will perform about 50 Europa flybys as it zips around the Jovian system, allowing it to map the moon's interior and work out the extent of its subsurface ocean while also studying other targets. "Putting an orbiter around Europa, because of the radiation environment, means you're only going to survive one to three months before the radiation kills you," says Curt Niebur, Europa *Clipper* program scientist at NASA Headquarters in Washington, D.C. "We realized instead we could fly by, collect our data and get the heck out of town where the radiation is lower. That way we can last years, not months."

During their overlapping missions, *JUICE* and *Clipper* will perform an intricate tango as they hop between Jupiter's attractions, with copious opportunities for collaboration. "To have two spacecraft in the same system will be really fantastic," Witasse says. About 20 scientists from both missions are meeting virtually every week as part of the *JUICE-Clipper* Steering Committee, with the group formulating ideas for how the two spacecraft might sync up at Jupiter. "We're busy talking through the science opportunities and coming up with a plan" to present to NASA and ESA, says Bunce, who co-chairs the committee with Prockter. Whereas "some of the details are a little bit different" from the initial EJSM collaboration, Bunce says, the overall dream remains alive. "The original plan was one mission focused on Ganymede and another mission focused on Europa," she says. "And that's what we've got."

One possibility is that each spacecraft could act as a spotter for the other. *JUICE*, for example, could keep an eye on Europa from afar as *Clipper* prepares to swoop past—a valuable partnership, especially if there are indeed plumes of liquid water spouting from cracks in the overlying ice. Peering into these plumes could lead to studying oceanic ejecta that are just "minutes old," Fox-Powell says. "It really gives us an opportunity to study something that's pristine." As *Clipper* approaches Europa, *JUICE* could look for plumes erupting from the surface, allowing *Clipper* to train its eye in that direction. "If *JUICE* spotted one, that could tell us where to look," Prockter says. *Clipper* may even fortuitously pass through some plumes, allowing it to directly sample them and look for signs of complex molecules that might hint at signs of life in the Europan ocean.

JUICE will perform two Europa flybys of its own prior to orbiting Ganymede. The one in July 2032 will be just four hours apart from a *Clipper* flyby. "We can make similar measurements at the same time," Witasse says. That could allow some exciting science to be done, although the exact details have yet to be determined. "We won't fly over the same location, but it will for sure be very interesting," he adds. "We could image similar surface features, or if there is a plume, we can observe it from different geometries."

The joint emphasis on Europa is partially based on scientists' suspicions that the moon's liquid-water ocean is in direct contact with a rocky core. There hydrothermal vents—openings in the seafloor where heat from deeper within can escape—could supply sufficient energy and nutrients to sustain life. "On Earth we have hydrothermal vents where there are whole communities of organisms," Fox-Powell says. "We have good reason to believe that similar kinds of chemical reactions are going on at Europa." Ganymede's much larger bulk, however, means that higher-density ice may have sunk to the bottom of its ocean, forming a vent-blocking barrier. "It could seal the rocky core away," Fox-Powell says. "Europa is not big enough to have that amount of gravity and pressure, so that high-pressure ice doesn't form."

Two Missions, One Vision

None of this rules out Ganymede's chances of habitability, nor does it diminish that moon's scientific interest. After entering orbit around Ganymede in December 2034, *JUICE* will survey the entire surface, study the moon's magnetic field and attempt to map its aquatic inner layers. For an environment to be interesting for potential habitability, it needs "a heat source, liquid water, organic material, and stability," Dougherty says. "At [Saturn's moon] Enceladus we know we've got three. At Europa we've got three. And at Ganymede we're trying to find out." Although it will start in a high orbit 5,000 kilometers above Ganymede, during a nine-month period *JUICE* will lower its altitude to just 200 kilometers over the moon's surface. Eventually, at the mission's end in 2035, the spacecraft will be deliberately crashed into the surface to minimize the chance of any debris contaminating Europa. Ganymede is not thought to have plume activity, but if it does or if its ice crust is found to be particularly thin, this finale may have to be rethought so as not to contaminate Ganymede's liquid ocean, too. "If there is something that indicates a connection with the inner ocean and the outer surface, we may need to change our orbit," says Giuseppe Sarri of ESA, project manager for *JUICE*.

Clipper will provide a similar level of knowledge about Europa and its ocean. It is not designed to find definitive evidence of life, however; at best, it will perhaps see the ingredients of life within the moon's plumes. Life detection may come on a later mission, such as NASA's much sought-after Europa Lander. A concept for the mission was drawn up years ago by scientists and engineers at NASA's Jet Propulsion Laboratory in California, but it awaits further funding. "Europa Lander has not been in the president's budget or the budget passed by Congress for a while," Niebur says. A road map for U.S. interplanetary exploration produced by the U.S. National Academies in late 2021, meanwhile, placed a Europa Lander mission as a lower priority for NASA than other projects.

For now the work is archived, ready and waiting to be reborn. "I'm confident that what Europa *Clipper* will learn will make us want to go back, and a lander of some kind is the logical next step," Niebur says. "But maybe Clipper will throw us a curveball, and a lander is not the right way to go. Maybe we'll want to hover in the plumes instead of landing."

If scientists do want to take a dip in this alien ocean, breaking through the kilometers-thick ice poses its own challenges. One possibility is that a lander could include a heat probe to melt its way through the frozen crust. Last year Paula do Vale Pereira, now at the Florida Institute of Technology, led an experiment to see how long that might take, using a two-meter-high column of cryogenic ice called the Europa Tower to simulate the Europan surface. Presenting her work at the 241st meeting of the American Astronomical Society in Seattle in early January 2023, she found the task might take anywhere between three and 13 years—long times to wait, even for multidecadal missions to the outer solar system.

Besides the ticking of the clock, other obstacles abound. "Figuring out a way to have cables transfer power and information between the lander and the probe is a big, big problem that needs to be solved in the coming years," do Vale Pereira says. The lander would have to carry perhaps several kilometers' worth of cable with it, and the cable would have to be resilient enough to endure water refreezing as ice around it during the probe's descent. The scientific value in solving such problems, however, is tremendous, not least the prospect of placing some kind of machine directly inside an alien ocean.

Such dreams are many years away. Any hope of making them a reality hinges on voyaging to Jupiter and confirming its icy moons are the attractive targets we believe them to be. Beginning with *JUICE* in April and *Clipper* next year, we are set to solve some of the most intriguing questions about Jupiter's moons that have long gone unanswered. The *Galileo* spacecraft "revealed to us that it's worth going back," Niebur says. Now we're doing so with not one but two spacecraft—a transatlantic partnership to significantly advance the search for habitability around our sun. There is no world in our solar system quite like Earth, but perhaps places like Europa and even Ganymede are a close second. If life can survive here, who knows where else it might thrive?

About the Author

Jonathan O'Callaghan is an award-winning freelance journalist covering astronomy, astrophysics, commercial spaceflight and space exploration. Follow him on X (formerly Twitter) @Astro_Jonny.

Mars Rovers Might Miss Signs of Alien Life, Study Suggests

By Derek Smith

F or most of the past half-century, scientists have been trying—and failing—to find life on Mars. Beginning with NASA's twin *Viking* landers, which touched down on the Red Planet in 1976, this hunt has focused on discovering possible biosignatures—organic molecules that may indicate life's past existence.

There are, of course, good reasons to suspect the search will ultimately prove successful. Although now inhospitably dry and cold, a wealth of evidence shows that Mars was once a warmer, wetter , and more habitable world. Life may have flourished there billions of years ago. Presumably, an epochal discovery could come from using a robot-borne chemistry lab to tease some telltale organic molecules out of an appropriate sample scoured from the right rock. But as highlighted in a recent study published in *Nature Communications*, this task may be too much for even our best present-day Mars explorers, NASA's *Curiosity* and *Perseverance* rovers. Perhaps evidence for life on Mars is hidden in plain view, merely unrecognized because of the limits of rocketry and current rover technology, and a breakthrough will only come if—or when—we manage to either bring bits of Mars back to Earth or send astronauts to the Red Planet.

The study was conducted by a team of international scientists led by Armando Azua-Bustos of the Center for Astrobiology in Spain. The researchers tested how well standard life-hunting technology could detect biosignatures not on Mars but rather right here on Earth. Using a series of instruments analogous to those on *Curiosity*, *Perseverance*, and the European Space Agency's upcoming *Rosalind Franklin* ExoMars rover, the team sought biosignatures in one of our planet's most Mars-like environments: the extremely arid Atacama Desert of the Chilean Andes. Specifically, they searched in the rust-colored, iron-rich sedimentary rocks that give the Atacama's Red Stone region its name. Some rover analogues could not detect any organics in the Red Stone rocks while others found potential biosignatures such as amino acids—but only after treating the samples with chemical reagents that are in short supply on current Mars rovers.

"Maybe we still need to do some work in order to detect evidence of life on Mars," Azua-Bustos says.

In some sense, the study is a validation of the current rovers on Mars. The team studied Red Stone samples with a roverlike kit, parts of which closely resemble the Sample Analysis at Mars (SAM) instrument onboard *Curiosity*, as well as a portion of *ExoMars*'s Mars Organic Molecule Analyzer (MOMA) instrument. Both tools heat rock and soil samples to vaporize organic molecules to gas, which is then sorted, fragmented, and weighed. These measurements produce a sort of "fingerprint" for various substances, allowing researchers to identify the types and abundances of molecules within a sample. Using their roverlike proxies, Azua-Bustos and his colleagues *did* find biosignatures in the Red Stone samples. But they only did so with the right treatments, detecting amino acids and carboxylic acids when the samples were treated with derivatizing reagents—chemicals that make certain organics vaporize more easily. These reagents are the only way to vaporize and thus detect some types of organic molecules with the heat treatments used by SAM and MOMA.

The trouble is that the threshold for using such derivatization reagents on Mars is exceedingly high. Like any consumable on an interplanetary mission, the reagents are only available in a very limited supply, just enough for a handful of attempts. *Curiosity*'s SAM only has nine single-use sample cups for derivatization. The *ExoMars* rover is similarly limited: it can only derivatize 12 samples, says Fred Goesmann, MOMA's principal investigator. Additionally, the reagents can linger in and around a rover's instrumentation, potentially contaminating unrelated samples. "That's why it took awhile to use [derivatization] on SAM," Goesmann adds. "Afterward your instrument is not as it was before," and cleaning it is difficult.

That's enough to make any mission planner think twice, especially because derivatization is perhaps best used on inherently marginal samples—those containing very low amounts of organic carbon that fail to reveal much when scrutinized with easier, more preliminary approaches. Although the study team did manage to use the technique to reveal otherwise-hidden organic molecules in some Red Stone samples, Goesmann says that because those samples were so marginal, "it's hard to say whether we would have decided to use derivatization right away" if the choice was being made for a rover on Mars.

In the Atacama, the team also tested techniques that are more analogous to *Perseverance*'s SuperCam and Scanning Habitable Environments with Raman and Luminescence for Organics and Chemicals (SHERLOC) instruments, which use different methods to detect organics. Those instruments measure how rocks fluoresce, absorb and reflect light when they are hit with different lasers. Certain minerals can also react to the laser light, however, and those abiotic mineral-sourced signals obscured fainter ones from organics in the Red Stone samples, Azua-Bustos says.

Besides finding potential flaws with current rover-borne instruments, the Red Stone study also field-tested technologies that presently do not have a rover analogue, with promising results. For example, the team successfully found faint traces of ancient cyanobacteria in Red Stone samples using the Signs of Life Detector, a device that relies on antibodies to detect specific organic compounds. This device is also less impacted by salts (abundant in Red Stone and Martian soils alike) that can degrade organics during the heat treatments used by SAM and MOMA.

"These kinds of instruments have been designed for planetary exploration, but they have not yet been applied to that," says Keyron Hickman-Lewis, a paleontologist at the Natural History Museum in London and a participating scientist in the *Perseverance* rover mission, who was not involved in the Red Stone study. The value of this study, he suggests, may be less in finding flaws in current techniques and more in vetting those that may someday be used in future missions.

In the end, each approach has its own strengths and weaknesses and is "seeing different things," Azua-Bustos says. No single instrument is likely to yield a conclusive detection of life. Instead only a collection of results from different analyses can provide a suitably comprehensive picture of any site's potential biosignatures. But including "all the things you can imagine here on Earth with teams across the world," he says, is a nonstarter for rovers because of their limited size, power supply, and operational lifetime.

Upscaled, far more sensitive versions of *Curiosity*'s SAM, for instance, can be the "the size of a room," which means they "are never going to be able to fly," says Mary Beth Wilhelm, an organic biogeochemist and planetary scientist at NASA's Ames Research Center, who was not involved in the study.

"Maybe rover technology is pushed to its limits by particularly subtle biosignatures," Hickman-Lewis says. "This is a good argument for Mars sample return." Fortunately, this is exactly the plan. NASA is leading an international effort to bring some Mars rocks to Earth by the early 2030s. It is already well underway: the *Perseverance* rover has filled around half of its sample tubes for eventual delivery back home.

Between Martian rocks brought to Earth and better organic-molecule-detecting instruments sent to Mars, the Red Planet's long-sought biosignatures are progressively running out of places to hide. That is presuming that they exist at all. Life may have never emerged on Mars. Of course, the only way to test that null hypothesis is to continue the search—ideally without overlooking any evidence that may lurk right under our robotic or real noses.

About the Author

Derek Smith is a freelance writer who tells stories about science and the natural world. His writing has appeared in Eos, Hakai Magazine, and institutional blogs. He has degrees in aquatic biology and environmental science.

NASA's *Perseverance* Rover May Already Have Evidence of Ancient Martian Life

By Jonathan O'Callaghan

I f life ever existed on Mars, we may already have the answer at hand. In January NASA's *Perseverance* rover deposited 10 tubes on the surface of Mars. Each contains a sample of Martian rock that was carefully selected for its potential to clarify chapters of the planet's still-murky history. Those tubes "are capable of telling us whether Mars was habitable," says Mitch Schulte, *Perseverance*'s program scientist at NASA Headquarters in Washington, D.C. "We see evidence of particular minerals that tell us there was water. Some of these minerals indicate there was organic material."

But to know for sure, scientists need to bring these tubes back to Earth for closer study—an audacious endeavor known as Mars Sample Return (MSR), which is slated for the early 2030s via a follow-up robotic mission. These 10 tubes are only the opening course in a bigger awaiting feast, a backup cache in case *Perseverance* breaks down before it can fill and deliver the 33 additional tubes that it carries. These tubes will hold samples sourced from the area in and around Jezero Crater, the site of a four-billion-year-old river delta and the locale where the rover landed on February 18, 2021. Although many of the samples are yet to be gathered for a journey to Earth that remains years in the future, those already collected have whetted researchers' appetite for their return home.

Scientists targeted Jezero for *Perseverance* because, on our planet, sprawling river systems like that found in the Martian crater build up enormous deposits of sediments. Washed in from a sizable swath of the surrounding landscape, these deposits contain various minerals that can be used to chart the Red Planet's past geology. Also most anywhere water is found on Earth, life accompanies it. The same might hold true for Mars, meaning Jezero's sediments could conceivably harbor biological remains. "We're looking for signs of habitability—liquid water and the raw materials of life," says Mark Sephton of Imperial College London, a member of the rover's sampling team.

Perseverance collects most of its samples using a small drill, producing chalk-stick-sized specimens that each fit within cigarlike tubes measuring less than 15 centimeters long. Of the 43 sample tubes, 38 are slated for samples from the surface, with the remaining five being "witness tubes" to catch whiffs of Martian air and check for any contaminating gases that might vent from the rover. Collected in September 2021, the rover's first sample is thought to be igneous rock from an ancient lava flow. Studying this material should allow scientists to date the crater more precisely. Since then, the rover has filled nearly half of its remaining tubes as it journeys several kilometers further up the ancient river's channels toward Jezero Crater's rim.

As a contingency, 10 of the samples are duplicates, each paired with another sample taken from the same location. These are the tubes *Perseverance* dropped on the surface as backup for potential future retrieval. In December 2022, in one of the last decisions he'd make at the space agency before reentering the private sector, NASA's then science chief Thomas Zurbuchen made the call to drop that cache at a location called Three Forks. The surface drop-off was completed at the end of January, around the same time *Perseverance* officially began the "extended" phase of its mission—and after the science team agreed that those 10 samples alone could answer the question of past habitability if needed. MSR's optimal plan calls for the rover to carry its remaining tubes to a yet-to-be-built lander slated to touch down in Jezero's vicinity around 2030. Once the lander has secured those samples, it will launch them on a rocket back to Earth.

"We want the ones on the rover to come back," Zurbuchen says. "But even the ones on the surface check all the boxes." That includes igneous rock to date the crater and sedimentary rock and clays that may contain biosignatures, perhaps even fossilized evidence of microbial life. "They're already worth the $10-billion investment," Zurbuchen says, citing the MSR program's estimated total cost. Some of the most promising samples are from a location called Wildcat Ridge, a meter-wide rock that contains evidence of sulfates. "Those are the ones we're most excited about in terms of potential biosignatures," says Kathleen Benison of West Virginia University, who is part of *Perseverance* 's sampling team. "Sulfate minerals can grow from groundwater. On Earth, those kinds of waters tend to have a lot of microbial life," which can be entombed and preserved in sulfate minerals.

Besides sulfates, life-seeking scientists are particularly eager to grab samples from mudstones—fine-grained sedimentary rocks that the *Curiosity* rover has seen in Gale Crater but that *Perseverance* has not yet spotted. "Microbe cells are tiny," says Tanja Bosak of the Massachusetts Institute of Technology, who is also part of the sampling team. "The mineral grain size should be even finer to preserve the [fossil] shape instead of destroying it. If you roll a boulder over a person, you will smush that person into something unrecognizable. For a microbe, *everything* is a boulder—unless you're talking about mudstones." The team members are also keen to sample carbonates, similar to things like chalk and limestone on Earth, which could preserve biosignatures as well. "If there had been microbial life in the lake, [the carbonates] could have trapped microbial matter in it," says Sanjeev Gupta of Imperial College London, who is one of the "long-term planners" who plot out the rover's path. On March 30, *Perseverance* collected its first carbonate sample, from a rock named "Berea" thought to have formed from material washed into Jezero by the ancient river.

While *Perseverance* has been hard at work collecting samples on Mars, the return phase of the mission remains in flux. Originally, NASA had planned for a European-built "fetch" rover to land on Mars around 2030, collect the samples from Perseverance and return them to a capsule on the lander for launch. Once in orbit, the sample capsule would rendezvous with a European orbiter, which would ferry the samples back to Earth for a landing in 2033. These plans were complicated, however, by Russia's invasion of Ukraine in

2022. In response to Russia's aggression, European Space Agency (ESA) officials chose to step back from a partnership with the nation on another long-simmering Mars mission, the *Rosalind Franklin ExoMars* rover. Russia had been due to provide the rover's nuclear power source, as well as the launch vehicle and landing platform. NASA has now agreed to supply such missing pieces and has sought funding to do so in its budgetary request to Congress last month. But this unanticipated assistance comes at the cost of the fetch rover. "We couldn't do both," Zurbuchen says. "We could not individually land the fetch rover and do *ExoMars*."

The ExoMars mission, most everyone agrees, is eminently worth saving. The *Rosalind Franklin* rover will carry a drill that can augur two meters beneath the Martian surface, accessing a subterranean habitat for past and present life that is considerably less hostile than the surface. "Nobody has ever done that on Mars," Zurbuchen says. "Our science community thinks it's really important."

Jorge Vago, ESA's ExoMars project scientist in the Netherlands, was glad that NASA stepped in. To hit a target launch date of 2028, set forth by European member states in order to save the mission, "we need the American contributions," Vago says. "It's an amazing mission. If we find super interesting stuff that's suggestive of a possible biological origin, I would expect we may want to have another sample return mission and bring back samples from the subsurface."

NASA's current MSR plan faces its own challenges. In a mid-March town hall hosted by NASA's Science Mission Directorate, Jeff Gramling, MSR program director at NASA Headquarters, said that some aspects of the mission may need to be "descoped." This would be a preventative measure to keep budgets under control. NASA's annual request of nearly $1 billion for MSR is expected to grow in the next few years, raising fears that unchecked increases could force the space agency to siphon funds from unrelated missions. Descoping options include removing one of two "Marscopters" planned for MSR, which had been included to build on the wildly successful *Ingenuity* rotorcraft that is now approaching 50 flights on Mars. Among other tasks, MSR's helicopters were added as a backup option for collecting the 10-tube sample cache at Three Forks. "The mission remains complex," Gramling said during the town hall. "We're working to our earliest possible launch date."

Despite the overwhelmingly intricate logistics of seeking life on Mars, the scientific riches on offer have lost none of their luster. *Perseverance*'s returned samples will cumulatively be only about half a kilogram, but the weight of their implications is immeasurable. Will they reveal that a second genesis of life in the universe has unfolded on the surface of Mars? For that matter, will *Rosalind Franklin*, once it arrives, validate the long-held suspicion that Mars's subsurface was—or still is—habitable, too? In our winding quest to determine if we are alone in the universe, the answer may be practically within our grasp, merely waiting for us to reach out to claim it. "We won't know until we get the samples back," Bosak says.

About the Author

Jonathan O'Callaghan is an award-winning freelance journalist covering astronomy, astrophysics, commercial spaceflight and space exploration. Follow him on X (formerly Twitter) @Astro_Jonny.

Martian Crust Could Sustain Life through Radiation

By Nikk Ogasa

Deep below the ground, radioactive elements disintegrate water molecules, producing ingredients that can fuel subterranean life. This process, known as radiolysis, has sustained bacteria in isolated, water-filled cracks and rock pores on Earth for millions to billions of years. Now a study published in *Astrobiology* contends that radiolysis could have powered microbial life in the Martian subsurface.

Dust storms, cosmic rays and solar winds ravage the Red Planet's surface. But belowground, some life might find refuge. "The environment with the best chance of habitability on Mars is the subsurface," says Jesse Tarnas, a planetary scientist at NASA's Jet Propulsion Laboratory and the new study's lead author. Examining the Martian underground could help scientists learn whether life could have survived there—and the best subsurface samples available today are Martian meteorites that have crash-landed on Earth.

Tarnas and his colleagues evaluated the grain sizes, mineral makeup and radioactive element abundance in Martian meteorites and estimated the Martian crust's porosity using satellite and rover data. They plugged these attributes into a computer model that simulated radiolysis to see how efficiently the process would have generated hydrogen gas and sulfates: chemical ingredients that can power the metabolism of underground bacteria. The researchers report that if water was present, radiolysis in the Martian subsurface could have sustained microbial communities for billions of years—and perhaps still could today.

Scientists have previously studied Mars radiolysis, but this marks the first estimate using Martian rocks to quantify the planet's subsurface habitability. Tarnas and his colleagues also evaluated the potential richness of life in the Martian underground and found that as many as a million microbes could exist in a kilogram of rock. (Geobiologists have found comparable densities in Earth's subsurface.)

The most habitable meteorite samples analyzed appeared to be made of a rock type called regolith breccia. "These are thought to come from the southern highlands of Mars, which is the most ancient terrain on Mars," Tarnas says.

Underground life, as described by this research, would require water—and it remains unknown if groundwater exists on the planet, says Lujendra Ojha, a planetary scientist at Rutgers University, who was not involved in the study. Determining whether the Martian crust contains water will be an important next step, but this investigation helps to motivate that search, Ojha says: "Where there is groundwater, there could be life."

About the Author

Nikk Ogasa is a California-based science journalist with a fondness for the environment, Earth and space, and a former editorial intern at Scientific American. *Follow Ogasa on X (formerly Twitter) @nikkogasa.*

Section 2: An Eye on UFOs

Here's What I Learned as the U.S. Government's UFO Hunter

By Sean Kirkpatrick

C arl Sagan popularized the maxim that "extraordinary claims require extraordinary evidence." This advice should not be optional for policy makers. In today's world of misinformation, conspiracy-driven decision-making, and sensationalist-dominated governance, our capacity for rational, evidence-based critical thinking is eroding, with deleterious consequences for our ability to effectively deal with multiplying challenges of ever increasing complexity.

As director of the Department of Defense's All-Domain Anomaly Resolution Office (AARO), charged by Congress in 2022 to help bring science-based clarity and resolution to the long-standing mystery surrounding credible observations of unidentified anomalous phenomena (UAP), also known as UFOs, I experienced this erosion up close and personal. And it was one factor in my decision to step down from my position last December. After painstakingly assembling a team of highly talented and motivated personnel and working with them to develop a rational, systematic and science-based strategy to investigate these phenomena, our efforts were ultimately overwhelmed by sensational but unsupported claims that ignored contradictory evidence yet captured the attention of policy makers and the public, driving legislative battles and dominating the public narrative.

The result of this whirlwind of tall tales, fabrication, and secondhand or thirdhand retellings of the same, was a social media frenzy and a significant amount of congressional and executive time and energy spent on investigating these so-called claims—as if we didn't have anything better to do.

The conspiracists' story goes something like this: The U.S. has been hiding and attempting to reverse engineer as many as 12 UAP/UFOs from as early as the 1960s and perhaps earlier. This great cover-up and conspiracy failed to produce any salient results, and consequently the effort was abandoned to some private sector defense contractors to continue the work. Sometime later, the story continues, those private sector contractors wanted to bring the whole program back under U.S. government (USG) auspices. Apparently, the CIA stopped this supposed transfer back to the USG. All of this is without substantiating evidence, but, alas, belief in a statement is directly proportional to the volume in which it is transmitted and the number of times it is repeated, not the actual facts.

During a full-scale, year-long investigation of this story (which has been told and retold by a small group of interconnected believers and others with possibly less than honest intentions—none of whom have firsthand accounts of any of this), AARO discovered a few things, and none were about aliens.

First, no record exists of any president or living DOD or intelligence community leader knowing about this alleged program, nor any congressional committee having such knowledge. This should speak volumes if this case were following typical procedure because it is inconceivable that a program of such import would not ever have been briefed to the 50 to 100 people at the top of the USG over the decades of its existence.

Second, this narrative has been simmering for years and is largely an outgrowth of a former program at the DOD's Defense Intelligence Agency (DIA) called the Advanced Aerospace Threat Identification Program (AATIP), which was heavily influenced by a group of individuals associated with businessman and longtime ufologist Robert Bigelow, founder of Bigelow Aerospace. In 2009 then-senator Harry Reid asked the secretary of defense (SECDEF) to set up a SAP (special access program) to protect the alleged UAP/UFO material that AATIP proponents believed the USG was hiding. The SECDEF declined to do so after a review by the Office of the Undersecretary of Defense for Intelligence (OUSDI), and DIA concluded that not only did no such material exist, but taxpayer money was being inappropriately spent on paranormal research at Skinwalker Ranch in Utah. This is well documented in open sources, particularly in records available on DIA's electronic FOIA Reading Room. After the negative response by SECDEF, Senator Reid then enlisted the help of then senator Joseph Lieberman to request that the Department of Homeland Security (DHS) set up an SAP for the same purpose. The administrative SAP proposal package was informed by the same individuals who had been associated with AATIP. AARO's archival research has located the administrative proposal for the DHS SAP, complete with the participants, which has been declassified and is being reviewed for public release.

Finally, the key purveyors of this narrative have known one another for decades. In the early 2000s several members of this small group also participated in a study, erroneously characterized (by the same participants) as having been sponsored by the White House, on the possible societal impact of disclosing the existence of extraterrestrials to the public, with the authenticity of the abovementioned concealed government program taken as its baseline assumption. The think tank in question was a "futures" enterprise that often worked on fringe studies, and many of the individuals involved with the study also worked for Bigelow Aerospace in support of the AATIP program.

AARO thoroughly investigated these claims as part of its congressionally mandated mission to not only technically evaluate contemporary UAP observations but also review historical accounts going back to the 1940s. One of my last acts before retiring was to sign AARO's *Historical Record Report Volume 1*, which is currently being prepared for delivery to Congress and the public. The report demonstrates that many of the circulating allegations described above derive from inadvertent or unauthorized disclosures of legitimate U.S. programs or related R&D that have nothing to do with extraterrestrial issues or technology. Some are misrepresentations, and some derive from pure, unsupported beliefs. In many respects, the narrative is a textbook example of circular reporting, with each person relaying what they heard, but the information often ultimately being sourced to the same small group of individuals.

The operational mission Congress has assigned AARO is important. Accumulating observations by highly trained U.S. military and other credible personnel of unidentified anomalous phenomena at or near sensitive national security areas and activities calls for a serious effort to understand what's going on. Simply put, "unidentified" is unacceptable, particularly in these times of heightened geopolitical tension. Part of the problem we face today, however, is that the modern media cycle drives stories faster than sound research, science, and peer review timelines can validate them. More worrisome is the willingness of some to make judgments and take actions on these stories without having seen or even requested supporting evidence, an omission that is all the more problematic when the claims are so extraordinary. Some members of Congress prefer to opine about aliens to the press rather than get an evidence-based briefing on the matter. Members have a responsibility to exhibit critical thinking skills instead of seeking the spotlight. As of the time of my departure, none, let me repeat, none of the conspiracy-minded "whistleblowers" in the public eye had elected to come to AARO to provide their "evidence" and statement for the record despite numerous invitations. Anyone that would rather be sensationalist in the public eye than bring their evidence to the one organization established in law with all of the legal process and security framework established to protect them, their privacy, and the information and to investigate and report out findings is suspect.

I can assure you as its former director that AARO is unwaveringly committed to harnessing science and technology to bring unprecedented clarity to these fascinating, important, and stubborn mysteries and to do so with maximum transparency. Its talented staff and team of supporting scientists are at this very moment striving in collaboration with the armed forces, intelligence community, government agencies, national laboratories, scientific community, academic community—and soon the general public—to collect and analyze hard, measurable data—i.e., extraordinary evidence—in this heretofore eyewitness-rich but data-poor field. The AARO team will go wherever the data takes it, without fail, and will not be swayed by any attempts to influence its findings otherwise. Science cannot be left on the side of the road in the mad dash to uncover some great conspiracy. Carl Sagan would expect no less, and neither should the American people.

This is an opinion and analysis article, and the views expressed by the author or authors are not necessarily those of Scientific American.

About the Author

Sean Kirkpatrick recently retired from federal service as the first director of the All-Domain Anomaly Resolution Office at the U.S. Department of Defense. He holds a Ph.D. in physics from the University of Georgia.

UFO Research Is Only Harmed by Antigovernment Rhetoric

By Marek N. Posard and Caitlin McCulloch

As the U.S. heads into another contentious election cycle, there is a glimmer of bipartisanship on Capitol Hill on an unexpected topic: unidentified anomalous phenomena.

That's right, UAPs—more commonly called UFOs.

Both Republicans and Democrats in Congress support efforts to make more government records related to UAPs open to the public. This is a productive step to begin looking at a whole host of terrestrial explanations for UAPs—everything from Chinese surveillance balloons to people putting guns on a drone—which is particularly welcome on a topic where research often lacks strong footing in scientific data.

However, this increased transparency—and any corresponding spotlight on UAPs—could take a dark turn if policy makers aren't careful.

Last year, the U.S. Department of Defense stood up the All-domain Anomaly Resolution Office (AARO), and it recently started to present data on its website. There's also support across the aisle in the Senate for an amendment to the National Defense Authorization Act that would create an independent board to declassify government UAP records. And NASA's UAP Independent Study Team just recommended a whole-of-government framework to collect high-quality data on these phenomena.

In theory, this should open the door to an objective and scientific approach to UAPs. But if the information release is haphazard, with a focus on one-off reports of sightings, that could backfire. U.S. national security agencies could suffer damage to their reputation. Those who work on, or report, such phenomena could be stigmatized.

Many in the American public feel a personal connection to the topic. Recent surveys find that about one quarter of Americans

39

report having seen some kind of UFO. Research we worked on at the nonprofit, nonpartisan RAND Corporation has found clusters of UFO reports across most U.S. states over the past several decades. These constituencies—and their elected officials—can be expected to have strong feelings about UAP data and what it does or doesn't show.

But there is also an undercurrent of conspiracy theory and, relatedly, antigovernment sentiment brewing around the issue. If this grows, it could prove toxic to any factual and scientific discussion of UAPs.

In July, the testimony during the House Oversight Committee's hearing on the issue included claims of a vast conspiracy by the U.S. Department of Defense, U.S. intelligence agencies, and their contractors to conceal evidence of extraterrestrials. There were accusations that government officials threatened witnesses with physical harm. In response, government officials have spoken out, calling some of these claims insulting to those serving in the national security establishment.

If UAP information gets caught up in debates over antigovernment conspiracies, that'll put the entire area of research—and the movement to make data more transparent—at risk.

For decades, the federal government and intelligence agencies have escalated public information sharing—but this has not produced a shared understanding of facts and events ranging from the attacks on 9/11 to the origins of COVID-19. Instead, intelligence agencies have found themselves under public attack and their findings dismissed. If it happens again, it could not only diminish morale among those working on UAPs, but also decrease governmental willingness to share information.

Antigovernment rhetoric can also sow public distrust. Public confidence in major U.S. institutions is already low. Surveys find that only 8 percent of Americans have confidence in Congress and 26 percent in the White House. About 60 percent report confidence in the U.S. military.

These institutions will play key roles in improving transparency about UAPs, and ultimately destigmatizing discussion of the issue and reports of sightings. Hopefully in the future, the institutions will also be able to rely on the public to report legitimate sightings. Such reporting will increasingly matter as more people, companies and countries start flying more things in the sky.

The creation of AARO last year, NASA's Unidentified Anomalous Phenomena Independent Study, and the proposed UAP Records Review Board are steps toward destigmatizing the issue. But this progress could end up derailed if the policy conversation gets mired in conspiratorial claims.

This is an opinion and analysis article, and the views expressed by the author or authors are not necessarily those of Scientific American.

About the Authors

Marek N. Posard is a military sociologist at the nonprofit, nonpartisan RAND Corporation and an affiliate faculty member at the Pardee RAND Graduate School.

Caitlin McCulloch is an associate political scientist at the RAND Corporation.

How Wealthy UFO Fans Helped Fuel Fringe Beliefs

By Keith Kloor

In a 2017 interview with *60 Minutes*, Robert Bigelow didn't hesitate when he was asked if space aliens had ever visited Earth. "There has been and is an existing presence, an ET presence," said Bigelow, a Las Vegas-based real estate mogul and founder of Bigelow Aerospace, a company NASA had contracted to build inflatable space station habitats. Bigelow was so certain, he indicated, because he had "spent millions and millions and millions" of dollars searching for UFO evidence. "I probably spent more as an individual than anybody else in the United States has ever spent on this subject."

He's right. Since the early 1990s, Bigelow has bankrolled a voluminous stream of pseudoscience on modern-day UFO lore—investigating everything from crop circles and cattle mutilations to alien abductions and UFO crashes. Indeed, if you name a UFO rabbit hole, it's a good bet the 79-year-old tycoon has flushed his riches down it.

But it's also a good bet that Bigelow would see this differently. After all, both the media and Congress are now solemnly discussing a supposed massive UFO cover-up by the U.S. government. There's even proposed legislation to open the X-Files! "The American public has a right to learn about technologies of unknown origins, non-human intelligence, and unexplainable phenomena," Senate Majority Leader Chuck Schumer of New York harrumphed in a recent public statement.

This legacy of plutocrat-backed fringe science comes as political partisanship, corporate propaganda, and conspiracy mongering continues to sow distrust in science. One lawmaker, Representative Tim Burchett of Tennessee, recently said, "The devil's been in our way," claiming a "cover-up" of UFO reports by military and intelligence agencies.

Such talk was once solely the domain of internet fever swamps and late-night conspiracy- themed radio shows. Now it's part of the political mainstream. This doesn't happen without Bigelow (and other wealthy eccentrics) greasing the way with their fat wallets. For example, Laurance Rockefeller was undoubtedly the most prominent UFO benefactor in the 1990s. The wealthy heir financed numerous UFO panels, conferences and, book-length reports that kept flying saucers in the public discourse.

From a scientific standpoint, all this money seems wasted on a zany quest that is akin to the search for Bigfoot or Atlantis. The same might be said of Harvard astrophysicist Avi Loeb's recent hunt for evidence of extraterrestrial life off the coast of Papua New Guinea, which cost $150,000 and was funded by cryptocurrency mogul Charles Hoskinson. Loeb's polarizing claims of finding traces of alien technology and of having a more open-minded and dispassionate approach to fringe science have garnered a truly staggering amount of media coverage, but his peers in the scientific community are rolling their eyes.

It's the latest stunt by Loeb, who also helms a controversial UFO project and previously drew the ire of his colleagues with outlandish claims about the supposedly artificial nature of an (admittedly weird) interstellar comet. Steve Desch, an astrophysicist at Arizona State University, recently told the *New York Times*: "What the public is seeing in Loeb is not how science works. And they shouldn't go away thinking that."

True, but as communication researcher Alexandre Schiele wrote in a 2020 paper for the *Journal of Science Communication,* what people see about "science" is usually on TV, particularly via sensationalist programming on cable channels such as Discovery and the misnamed History Channel, where viewers are "bombarded with aliens, ghosts, cryptids, and miracles as though they are indisputable facts."

Unfortunately, much of this nonsense has, at one point or another, been masked with an aura of legitimacy by prestigious institutions. For example, the Massachusetts Institute of Technology lent its imprimatur to an alien abduction conference in the early 1990s—which Robert Bigelow helped pay for. A generous benefactor to academia, Bigelow also gave millions to the University of Nevada during the 1990s to study supposed psychic phenomena, such as telepathy, clairvoyance, and the possibility of life after death. (In recent years, the billionaire has turned his attention and money largely to the afterlife.)

Indeed, there is a long tradition of fringe science at prestigious universities. The dubious field of parapsychology, for instance, owes its existence to the decades of pseudoscholarship churned out at Duke and Harvard University—and financed by wealthy private patrons. Some of our most illustrious thinkers, such as the eminent psychologist William James, have fallen for it. Belief in Martians sprang in large part from a wealthy amateur astronomer, Percival Lowell, who built the observatory that still bears his name. A University of Arizona psychology professor attracted criticism in recent years for taking money from the Pioneer Fund, founded in 1937 by textiles magnate to promote the racist science of eugenics.

Eventually, this wacky stuff, be it ESP or UFOs, makes its way to Congress and the Pentagon. That's how we end up with people in government-funded programs who claim they can bend spoons with their minds or walk through walls. And that's how we end up with the Department of Defense giving Robert Bigelow $22 million from 2008 to 2011 to investigate UFOs, werewolves, and poltergeists (seriously) on a Utah ranch.

This would be the same ranch Bigelow had already bought after reading a story in a Utah newspaper about how the property was teeming with UFOs, including one "huge ship the size of several football fields."

Does this sound familiar? If so, that's because in recent weeks, a number of similar hard-to-fathom, evidence-free UFO claims have echoed without challenge through the halls of Congress and all over television networks. Among the most eyebrow raising: tales of recovered saucers, hidden alien bodies, and a football field–sized UFO spotted over a military base.

Guess what: You can draw a line from these outlandish assertions to the vast repository of so-called studies once funded by Bigelow. In fact, some of the people he contracted to write them, such as astrophysicist Eric Davis, have acknowledged speaking (behind closed doors) with Congress.

To say UFO enthusiasm has swept Washington D.C. is not an overstatement. In recent years, there have been three Congressional hearings and two Pentagon task forces. NASA is about to deliver its own verdict after a year-long study. As Timothy Noah writes in the New Republic, "UFOs are fast becoming the most-studied topic in American governance."

Perhaps, but Robert Bigelow will tell you that nobody has studied the topic more than him. He might be right. Whatever the latest UFO whistleblower says and whatever Congress turns up, you can bet that Bigelow already paid for it.

This is an opinion and analysis article, and the views expressed by the author or authors are not necessarily those of Scientific American.

About the Author

Keith Kloor is New York City–based journalist and adjunct professor of journalism at New York University.

Bad Data, Not Aliens, May Be behind UFO Surge, NASA Team Says

By Leonard David

G aining any new clarity about surging reports of unidentified anomalous phenomena, or UAP, will take time, better data gathering and diagnostic tools and, perhaps most importantly, a hale and hearty dose of nit-picking scientific scrutiny. It may also require a better, sharper definition of what "anomalous" even means in the context of recent sightings.

At least, that's the emerging conclusion of a NASA-chartered, blue-ribbon panel of 16 independent experts who span a number of scientific and technical communities. The team, which was convened last year, is continuing to work toward a report to be published later this summer. But in a recent public briefing, it offered its first-cut verdict on ways to empirically grapple with the slippery subject of UAP.

Astrophysicist David Spergel, president of the Simons Foundation and a professor emeritus at Princeton University, chairs the effort, which is officially called the Unidentified Anomalous Phenomena Independent Study. At the outset of the May 31 meeting, Spergel set the tone: today's existing data and eyewitness reports are insufficient to yield conclusive evidence about the nature and origin of every UAP event, he said, primarily because of a lack of quality control and poor data curation.

One idea already bandied about by the panel is a permanent office within NASA to collate and archive UAP information.

The group's overall goal is to craft a where-to-go-from-here roadmap on how NASA can contribute to UAP studies, tapping its unique position as a civilian agency that handles data from the heavens and Earth alike in an open and transparent manner. "NASA's responsibility is to listen to our advice, take it seriously and then assess which aspects of it they want to follow," Spergel said at the meeting.

Many of the UAP events can be attributed to commercial aircraft, drones, and research balloons, as well as weather and ionospheric phenomena, Spergel stated. "That said, there remain events that we do not understand. But these events tend to be characterized by poor quality and limited data," he added.

Novel Physical Phenomenon

Might there be riches untold awaiting anyone who successfully cracks the nature of UAP?

At the meeting, Spergel said the history of fast radio bursts is instructive. When these brief, powerful blips were first seen in data from radio telescopes, many skeptics suspected they would be traced to mundane, terrestrial electromagnetic interference of one kind or another. Instead further examination confirmed the bursts were cosmic in nature, emerging from astrophysical cataclysms scattered across the universe. "Sometimes anomalies are really interesting and point to novel physical phenomenon. I think there's a number of interesting lessons learned there," he said.

Likewise, Spergel singled out sprites—mysterious sprawling flashes of light that commercial pilots have reported seeing above intense thunderstorms. Early on, to some extent, sprites were simply dismissed as illusory before being found as authentic, albeit very strange. Spergel pointed out that it ultimately took high-speed imaging data, often from orbital assets such as the International Space Station, to learn about the true nature of these intriguing ionospheric occurrences: they are essentially upward-moving discharges of lightning.

"I think this is one of the fascinating things about the UAP phenomenon," Spergel said. "If it's something that's anomalous, that makes it interesting and worthy of study."

Spergel added that panel members have suggested ways to engage citizen scientists. For example, given that several billion cell phones are in use around the globe, those devices not only record sounds and images but also gauge local magnetic fields and provide good geospatial and temporal calibration via GPS.

NASA could enlist private companies to develop software apps designed to allow smartphones to record more and better UAP data, Spergel said. Such apps could then upload the crowdsourced data to a central repository for subsequent analysis. This and other ways of casting a wider net for UAP data help "eliminate the normal, then identify anything interesting," he said.

Similar in thought was panel member Federica Bianco, an astrophysicist and data scientist at the University of Delaware. At the meeting, she advocated crowdsourcing, harnessing a large and decentralized group of people to help dig into UAP, to tackle the issue.

Bianco cautioned, however, that the application of the scientific method to discovery requires that the UAP data meet rigorous standards—especially if any of that analysis will rely on automated processing by artificial intelligence and machine-learning tools.

Separate Fact from Fiction

The "Why now, why NASA?" question was underscored by Daniel Evans, assistant deputy associate administrator for research at NASA's Science Mission Directorate. He serves as the space agency official responsible for orchestrating the study.

Another goal of the group is to assess whether UAP pose any risks to safe operations in air and space, Evans explained. "And we're doing it using science," he said. "NASA believes that the tools of science apply to the study of UAP because they allow us to separate fact from fiction. And that's all part of NASA's commitment to exploring the unknown."

Evans said he wanted to emphasize loudly and proudly that "there is absolutely no convincing evidence for extraterrestrial life associated with UAPs." Nevertheless, trying to come to grips with the UAP enigma has sparked a predictable and palpable backlash.

Evans wouldn't get into specifics but did say that there has been online harassment of several study team members. Labeling it "disheartening," he said a NASA security team is actively addressing the issue. "If we are truly to approach UAP with an unwavering commitment and dedication to the scientific process, then harassment of any nature only serves to detract from that process," Evans said.

Everyday Characteristics

Sean Kirkpatrick is director of the U.S. Department of Defense's All-Domain Anomaly Resolution Office (AARO), established in 2022. Speaking before the panel, he emphasized that a very small percentage of UAP reports could reasonably be described as anomalous. The majority of unidentified objects reported to AARO and in its holdings—now a collection of more than 800 incidents—demonstrate everyday characteristics of readily explainable sources, such as aircraft, balloons, and even litter wafting through the atmosphere.

But there are head-scratching UAP reports, Kirkpatrick added, primarily because of a lack of data associated with those cases. "Without sufficient data, we are unable to reach defendable conclusions that meet the high scientific standards we set for resolution," he said.

Meanwhile Kirkpatrick said that for the few objects that do display potentially anomalous characteristics, "AARO is approaching these cases with the highest level of objectivity and analytical rigor." To that end, he reported that the office is deploying "purpose-built surveillance systems" to understand "what's normal and what's not normal" in the perplexing world of UAP.

Evidence-Based Knowledge

Harvard University astrophysicist Avi Loeb is on the same UAP page as the NASA panel, which he isn't a part of. Loeb is leader of the

Galileo Project, an effort focused on finding and carefully studying anomalous objects using the best scientific tools available. That initiative has designed, built, and fielded sensitive sensor gear—often mated to sizable telescopes—to opportunistically capture sonic, spectral, and radar data from UAP.

"Government agencies and academia should be working collaboratively towards the scientific collection of evidence-based knowledge on truly anomalous objects near Earth," Loeb wrote in a post-NASA-panel-meeting essay. He added that, overall, the panel's outcome was a "win-win" development and that a hunt for out of the ordinary objects should be based on "seeking new data agnostically with well-calibrated and controlled instruments."

Mick West, a former video game programmer and noted skeptic, who is also not a panel member, says he was heartened to see detailed looks of purported UAP caught on video.

"There was a strong emphasis on the need for calibrated data. This means that they don't think the existing videos [of UAP] are particularly useful, as they were not captured with calibrated instruments," West says. He concurs with those taking part in the NASA UAP study who see eyewitness accounts as not very useful beyond establishing patterns of event locations—and agrees that, as of yet, none of the available evidence points to extraterrestrial origins for any UAP.

UAP Terminology

Robert Powell gives a thumbs-up to the idea of a permanent NASA UAP program. Powell is an executive board member of the nonprofit Scientific Coalition for UAP Studies (SCU), a think tank of scientists, past military officers, and other professionals and is not on the panel. SCU was formed in August 2017 and has been steadfast in studying the enigma of UAP and calling for more rigorous research on the phenomena since that time.

UAP investigations should not fall exclusively under the auspices of the DOD, Powell contends. The agency has a different set of fundamental interests that do not include open data and public science, he advises.

"If a portion of what we call UAP is caused by an unknown intelligence of unknown origin, I can think of no more qualified group than NASA to make that determination," Powell says.

Eager to provide guidance, Powell does sense a need to tighten up UAP terminology. One of the first steps that NASA should take is to describe exactly what is meant by "anomalous maneuvers" and precisely what is meant by "evidence of an extraterrestrial presence," he says.

"Until criteria are established that state exactly how measuring equipment will determine an aerial object is controlled by an extraterrestrial intelligence, then no claims as to the existence or lack of existence of extraterrestrials should be made," Powell says. "There is nothing wrong with saying, 'We don't yet know.' "

Words Matter

Does the term "UAP" tarnish long-held folklore that swirls around unidentified flying objects (UFOs)—stories of crashed flying saucers, recovered hardware and even occupants, all secreted by government cover-ups? Do UAP perhaps have nothing to do with the possibility of other star folk visiting Earth?

In an interview with *Scientific American*, panel member Mike Gold, chief growth officer at Redwire Space and former associate administrator for Space Policy and Partnerships at NASA, said the use of "UAP" was intended to get away from the assumptions and baggage that are part of the term "UFO".

Speaking as an admitted "recovering attorney," Gold told *Scientific American*, "I believe words matter.... Words have power. What we're trying to do with this group is to be agnostic, to be objective, and to look at this issue purely from a scientific perspective, without bias."

Given that prescriptive outlook, the NASA-commissioned Unidentified Anomalous Phenomena Independent Study is raising a "we're from the government, and we're here to help" flag while sanctifying a scientific look at aerial weirdness. It does so at a time when skeptical forces hold tight to their view that, at least when it comes to aliens, a long and checkered history of confirmed or rumored cover-ups renders any official statement from the U.S. government inherently untrustworthy.

In the end, how the panel's report is publicly embraced may, just like UAP, be up in the air.

About the Author

Leonard David is author of Moon Rush: The New Space Race *(National Geographic, 2019) and* Mars: Our Future on the Red Planet *(National Geographic, 2016). He has been reporting on the space industry for more than five decades.*

To Understand UAP, We Need Megapixel Imagery

By Avi Loeb

The Pentagon report on unidentified aerial phenomena (UAP) that was delivered to Congress on June 25 is intriguing enough to motivate scientific inquiry towards the goal of what these phenomena are. The nature of UAP is not a philosophical matter. It's also not a puzzle that politicians should be asked to resolve—for the same reason that plumbers should not be asked to bake cakes. Policy makers or military personnel have insufficient training in science to solve this mystery, and hoping that they will somehow do so is like the frustrating experience of the characters in Samuel Beckett's play *Waiting for Godot*.

Given these circumstances, scientists should find the answer through the standard scientific process, based on a transparent analysis of open data. The task boils down to getting a high-resolution image of UAP. A picture is worth a thousand words. More specifically, a megapixel image of the surface of an unusual object will allow us to distinguish whether it bears the metaphorical label "Made in China" or "Made in Russia" from the alternative: "Made on Exoplanet X."

Consider an object the size of a person at a distance of one mile. Suppose we wish to resolve features as small as the width of a letter in this text. That is equivalent to resolving a thousandth of the person's height, which would require obtaining a megapixel image. The Rayleigh criterion in optics implies that the best angular resolution of a telescope is at the so-called "diffraction limit," roughly the wavelength of light divided by the aperture diameter. For visible light, the desired resolution in our example can be obtained by a telescope with a diameter of a meter, which can be purchased off-the-shelf online.

The telescope should be linked to a suitable camera, with the resulting data stream fed to a computer system—where optimized software would filter out the transients of interest as the telescope tiles the sky with its field of view. The initial survey could start from a large field of view, but then zoom in on the object of interest as it is tracked across the sky. UAP could change their sky position much faster than any astronomical sources located at great distances.

But they also need to be distinguished from birds, airplanes, satellites, or instrumental artifacts. The actual fidelity of the image will be limited by blurring owing to atmospheric turbulence and will therefore depend on the elevation and distance of the UAP. The sky survey will also need to extend over a period of time long enough for the detection of UAP to be probable. These are all major challenges.

The telescope facilities can be placed in geographical locations that will maximize the chance of reproducing past UAP reports. Lower-cost video cameras with lower resolution can be distributed across more locations around the globe to achieve a comprehensive survey of the entire sky. There are astronomical facilities, such as ZTF, LCO, TAOS, ASASSN, or PanSTARRS, already in place at remote locations for the different task of searching for transient objects that do not move across the sky as fast as UAP. The data volume will increase dramatically when the VRO/LSST facility in Chile commences operations in 2023. UAP debunkers often ask why cameras invariably capture fuzzy images of unidentified objects. The answer is simple: their apertures are hundreds of times smaller than the desired meter-scale telescopes.

The cost of establishing a network of suitable telescopes is lower than the amount invested so far in the search for the nature of dark matter. We do not know which particles constitute most of the matter in the universe. It is a search compromised by uncertainties, just like the search for UAP. But if some of the UAP are of extraterrestrial origin, the implications would be far greater for society than proving that dark matter is weakly interacting massive particles (WIMPs) as opposed to something else. The extraterrestrial finding may well change the way we perceive our place in the universe, our aspirations for space, our theological and philosophical beliefs, and even the way we treat other humans.

And all of these implications can be triggered by a single megapixel image obtained at a reasonable cost. In a forum that I attended recently concerning my book *Extraterrestrial,* I was asked about the prior probability assigned to the possibility that the weird interstellar object 'Oumuamua or UAP are extraterrestrial in origin. I clarified that it is unknown just as in the case of dark matter being WIMPs. But since a megapixel image of UAP is affordable and is of great interest to the public and the government, we should simply obtain one. Indeed, a picture of an 'Oumuamua-like object would be worth 66,000 words—the number of words in my book. We should not seek data from government-owned sensors that were not designed for this purpose, but instead collect our own state-of-the-art scientific data in a reproducible fashion. Most of the sky above us is not classified.

In a podcast interview I recently had with a young audience, they agreed: "Let's just do it." It was refreshing to see eye-to-eye with the torch bearers of the future, as well as with potential funders of the UAP imaging project, all within the same week. A day later, I was asked by Rahel Solomon of CNBC: "How do you plan to celebrate UAP Day?" Thankful for the reminder, I said: "We will probably need our computers to figure out the nature of UAP, and so my plan is to celebrate the day with my computer."

This is an opinion and analysis article; the views expressed by the author or authors are not necessarily those of Scientific American.

About the Author

Avi Loeb is former chair (2011-2020) of the astronomy department at Harvard University, founding director of Harvard's Black Hole Initiative and director of the Institute for Theory and Computation at the Harvard-Smithsonian Center for Astrophysics. He also chairs the Board on Physics and Astronomy of the National Academies and the advisory board for the Breakthrough Starshot project, and is a member of President's Council of Advisors on Science and Technology. Loeb is the bestselling author of Extraterrestrial: The First Sign of Intelligent Life Beyond Earth *(Houghton Mifflin Harcourt).*

Chinese Spy Balloon Saga Shows UFOs Deserve Serious Investigations

By Mick West

A t latest count, Sidewinder missiles have burst both a wayward Chinese balloon and three "unidentified objects" floating over the U.S. and Canada. These suspected spies cast an unexpected spotlight on a significant national security issue: balloons and drones gathering intelligence for foreign powers.

But they also provide a likely explanation for some of the last decade's highly publicized sightings of unidentified flying objects by military pilots. At least a more plausible explanation than extraterrestrials. And the Pentagon's past habit of punting such observations to a quirky and inadequate team of investigators from an obscure task force was an institutional failure.

Although the first balloon burst, a 200-foot-high white sphere, was the opposite of stealthy or unidentified, the more recent aerial objects downed over Alaska, Canada, and Lake Huron, fell squarely in the realm of unidentified anomalous phenomena (UAP), the latest name for UFOs that the Pentagon settled on last year.

Birds, party balloons, weather balloons, and trash that might be labeled UAP fill the sky, along with drones, consumer and otherwise. We now know that the U.S.-Canada North American Aerospace Defense Command had blunted its radars to prevent such aerial flotsam from cluttering its screens, according to the White House. Until now, the priority targets were aircraft and missiles, which are large and fast. Small, slow objects, like balloons, were filtered out and ignored.

That's why we didn't know about the balloons that likely explain the "GoFast" UFO sighting made by U.S. Navy pilots in 2015, a seeming high speed encounter over the ocean that, in truth, depicts a much slower object made to look fast by the parallax effect, where the high speed is only relative to the Navy plane, like a tree "flying" past the window of a train. Balloons might even explain some aspects of the 2004 USS *Nimitz* "Tic Tac" incidents.

Now radars are looking for such objects. That's why pilots are seeing—and shooting down—UAP. Descriptions of the UAP encountered by some Navy pilots also tally with aspects of newly revealed incursions of Chinese balloons during the Trump administration. *Politico* reported that intelligence analysts assessed that some small objects detected off the coast of Virginia were Chinese radar-jamming devices. This could correlate with multiple reports of erratic radar returns by pilots training in that area. One visual sighting described by pilots as a "cube in a sphere" is a close match for an inflatable radar decoy.

In observing the Pentagon's UAP task force and having done detailed analyses of several cases they struggled with, I find abundant reasons to doubt their capabilities to crack those kinds of UAP cases. A slide in a congressional briefing reportedly prepared by the task force head, John Stratton, according to a popular UFO podcast series, claimed to show "three UAP" hovering over a Navy ship. Those UAP were stars, I demonstrated last year, and their curious triangular shape was a camera artifact, a conclusion later confirmed in Congressional testimony. My analyses of other task force cases, involving gun camera footage of indistinct shapes, have also been supported by Pentagon sources cited by the *New York Times*.

The past mistakes matter, not only because the task force's initial attempts at identification failed but because that office was notable for its small size, dubious background in paranormal investigations (really), and poor record in not only failing to solve cases but sometimes getting them entirely wrong. This leads us to question how many other cases of foreign surveillance were swept under the rug as UAP.

How many other Chinese (or Russian or other) spy drones have military and intelligence officials sidelined as UFOs, rather than terrestrial threats? The first public report produced by the UAP task force in June 2021 listed 144 cases, of which they could only solve one with high confidence, identifying it as a large, deflating balloon (of unstated nationality). The remaining 143 presumably include the handful that were later identified as Chinese airspace incursions.

After the Pentagon restructured the task force into a new organization called the All-domain Anomaly Resolution Office with new personnel last year, a second report was released in January. The report added 366 new cases to the 143, but the number with a seeming explanation jumped from one to 195, with a majority of those, strangely enough, thought to be balloons. It is likely this was achieved by a new technique of reviewing archived raw radar footage, from which the slow-moving balloons (and a few drones) had previously been filtered out as "clutter."

While most were likely mundane airspace clutter such as mylar party balloons and consumer drones, some of them could represent Chinese intelligence-gathering platforms. It is unlikely we can resolve any historical cases as such, but when new balloons are detected, this could be determined by intercepting them, shooting them down, and examining the wreckage.

Some UFO enthusiasts initially leaped on the big Chinese balloon as an example of how foreign attempts at spying would be easily detected, concluding that it was evidence that the other reports of more ambiguous UFOs were not conventional human technology.

But subsequent developments point in the opposite conclusion: The big balloon was large and obvious. Smaller balloons and other aerial platforms have, both literally and figuratively, slipped under the radar for years. Senate Majority Leader Chuck Schumer of New York described the latest objects shot down as part of a worldwide "crew of balloons."

The Pentagon's new resolution office is doing better. But its establishment was still loosely rooted in a history of people hoping that UFOs are alien visitors—their proclamations sparking misdirected public uproar, despite a decades-long deficit of clear supporting evidence. The reality of persistent Chinese attempts at airspace intrusions and surveillance should lead the Pentagon to focus instead on the very real tasks at hand.

This is an opinion and analysis article, and the views expressed by the author or authors are not necessarily those of Scientific American.

About the Author

Mick West is a writer and retired software engineer. The author of Escaping the Rabbit Hole: How to Debunk Conspiracy Theories using Facts, Logic, and Respect, *he founded Metabunk.org, where he and others analyze and explain unusual claims, including UFO videos.*

Section 3: Communicating with Aliens

Can You Decode an Alien Message?

By Shi En Kim

W hat if aliens in the universe send a message to Earth, and we can't understand what they're saying? Communicating with another species is likely to be tricky, given how difficult it already is for humans from one culture and language to be understood by those from another. So how much harder might it be to bridge the gap between us and creatures whose bodies, minds, and habitats are completely foreign to ours?

To ponder the question and practice decoding an extraterrestrial epistle, an artist-led team has created a mock message from the stars to test us Earthlings. On May 24 the ExoMars Trace Gas Orbiter beamed the note from Mars toward Earth. Three observatories detected the transmission 16 minutes later: the Medicina Radio Observatory in Bologna, Italy; the Allen Telescope Array in northern California; and the Robert C. Byrd Green Bank Telescope in West Virginia. The message, though written for humans by humans, was as nonanthropocentric as one could hope for, perhaps the most alien missive the world had ever received.

This interplanetary art project, called A Sign in Space, is an ongoing experiment: for all of humanity's hopes for detecting technosignatures, do we have the chops to make sense of them? So far no one has deciphered the May 24 message, but many are on the case.

A Cosmic Letter

Only three people in the world know what A Sign in Space's message means. First among them is Daniela de Paulis, the project's founder and an artist in residence at the SETI Institute (SETI stands for the "search for extraterrestrial intelligence") and the Green Bank Observatory. She and two other co-authors penned the faux alien missive after consulting with poets, scientists, programmers, and philosophers.

Right away, de Paulis recognized the project's out-of-this-world dilemma: How could her team shed its anthropocentricity to craft a message that seemed as realistically alien as possible? The challenge wasn't just to think like an extraterrestrial but also to jettison Earth's regional biases. Her team immediately ruled out language-based communication, though she won't confirm or deny whether the message contains any text. Her team even agonized over using mathematics—although the fundamental concepts are universal, different societies may think about and represent math differently. Composing the message and choosing the right format gave de Paulis massive writer's block. "It was really very heavy work to dismantle our Western-centric thinking," she says.

De Paulis struggled with the message for years after she conceived the project in 2019. A breakthrough came in late 2022 when she contacted artist and computer programmer Giacomo Miceli, inadvertently recruiting the second author for the message. A month before the transmission deadline, astronomer Roy Smits joined the pair, adding a mathematical touch to make the message "more universal, so to speak," de Paulis says—and much harder to crack because it looks nothing like what humans use in our daily conversations.

People have constructed communiqués meant for extraterrestrials in the past. In 1974 scientists blared a radio message into the universe using the Arecibo Telescope in Puerto Rico. The interstellar postcard—a 1,679 string of 1's and 0's that, when translated graphically, consisted of crude representations of a human, the Arecibo Telescope's dish, and the DNA double helix, among others—was more symbolic than a genuine attempt to hail beings in space. The likelihood of this "Arecibo message" ever being understood by extraterrestrials is slim: when its composer, the late astronomer Frank Drake, gave the Arecibo message to his colleagues to interpret for fun, none of them succeeded.

That project, as well as the new experiment, illustrate just what a tall order true understanding between species is. "The beauty of A Sign in Space is to make us reflect on just how it is more frustratingly difficult and ultimately a much more profound sort of contact than Hollywood would ever portray," says Douglas Vakoch, president of the organization METI (Messaging Extraterrestrial Intelligence) International, who wasn't involved in the project. Though receiving an actual sign from aliens would be incredibly inspirational, what happens next might be less fun than movies suggest. "In the short term, it's going to be incredibly boring and frustrating," Vakoch says.

Message Extraction

From the first announcement, the project drew in an army of nerds and puzzle wonks. They flocked to Discord to exchange ideas, united by the belief that the message was ripe for solving.

One of the project's more than 4,700 subscribers on Discord is Gonzalo José Carracedo Carballal, a 34-year-old Ph.D. student in astrophysics at the Complutense University of Madrid. A radio astronomy devotee, he fills his spare time working on radio wave projects in a room littered with instruments and parts. A satellite dish peeks from his balcony. Tattooed on his right triceps is an excerpt from the etchings on the *Pioneer 10* and *11* probes' plaque—another 1970s attempt by Earth scientists to introduce our species to any space aliens that might encounter the craft.

Carracedo Carballal was part of the first group of people to extract the raw message from the ExoMars orbiter's broadcast. The communiqué was a 4.8-gigabyte string of numbers describing the waveform of the telemetry data, interwoven with the alien message. Unlike a real extraterrestrial note, which would arrive unannounced, this signal came in at a precisely scheduled time. Comparing the arrival timing with previous transmissions the telescopes received, the amateur code breakers identified a telltale data packet in the radio signal that was more active and sizable than usual. A week's effort of filtering the data segment, which Carracedo Carballal likens to peeling layers off an onion, eventually led to an 8.2-kilobyte bitmap image of five speckled clusters set against a blank background.

Soon after Carracedo Carballal and his colleagues found the raw message, speculations on its meaning erupted. Perhaps the message was hinting at the aliens' appearance, morse code, cellular automata or the genetic secrets of E.T. One user enlisted ChatGPT to reverse engineer a first-contact-appropriate message as a starting point. Several users suggested that the image was a star map broadcasting the civilization's location. Others proposed that the dots represented constellations of a much punier scale: molecules, perhaps the biosignatures of the foreign home world.

The raw message looked too random to be comprehensible. Decoding was necessary to wrangle it into a more intelligible form. But where to start was the infernal question; every attempt would be a stab in the dark. "You start to see patterns," Carracedo Carballal says of the process. "You have to stop and think whether something is actually there, or you're just projecting."

The Hard Part

Whenever Ivi Hasanaj, a 32-year-old software engineer based in Germany, starts to work on decoding A Sign in Space's message for the day, he opens up the raw image on his computer and stares. He stares and stares some more until an idea occurs to him, and he writes code to manipulate the image.

Hasanaj doesn't think aliens—or A Sign in Space's organizers—are the sadistic sort who would make message recipients bang their head for nothing more than private amusement. Messages are meant to be understood. Although he hadn't thought much about the problem of extraterrestrial communication before this project, Hasanaj has solved many puzzles on the gamified coding platform Codewars, and this experience comes in handy. For one, he recognizes the difference between decryption and decoding.

Decryption is the process of making sense of a concealed message for which only the intended recipient has a key, or a translation hack, to understand it. This kind of code breaking is much more difficult than decoding: the biggest hurdle is guessing the missing key.

On the other hand, a message with the key already embedded inside lends itself to decoding. When decoding, the user shouldn't introduce new information into the message. Any operation on the raw file, such as a rotation or an overlay, should come from instructions that the reader has managed to extract from the message. Otherwise it would be like arbitrarily rearranging the letters of a word to arrive at a new anagram.

Hasanaj isn't sure of the true content of A Sign in Space's message, but his own best guess is a numerical system that counts from one to five. He uncovered this from observing a recurring pattern among the brightest pixels in the image.

But he hasn't been able to account for the remaining flecks, which constitute the majority of the signal. Perhaps other kinds of information beyond math lurk in the message. He thinks no part of the already slim communication is redundant: aliens would probably make every pixel count. Whether or not he's on the right track, he says he'll know the correct answer when he sees it.

The community is still trying to decode the message—pursuing 30-some ideas for how to do so—before even attempting to interpret its full meaning. For this process, participants can take a less technical, and more cultural, approach to making sense of the message, as they might do for an abstract painting. For now, the signal is still too random to be interpretable. Watching their efforts unfold, de Paulis thinks these scattershot efforts may be distracting users from exploring each idea to the full. "They can't focus on one particular decision," she observes. "I think that's the main problem." If the public remains stuck on the decoding process, she says her team will likely organize an online hackathon later in August.

A Global Quest

Humanity's best shot at understanding an extraterrestrial message is to throw a consortium of diverse expertise at it, Vakoch says. A Sign in Space is a shining example of what that may look like. So far the project's eclectic group of volunteers have made impressive headway.

But in the event of a real extraterrestrial signal reaching Earth, the public isn't likely to be invited to help with the decoding process. In 1989 the International Academy of Astronautics established a postdetection protocol that largely emphasizes secrecy. The guidelines have had little updating since. "An international committee of scientists and other experts should be established to serve as a focal point for continuing analysis... and also to provide advice on the release of information to the public," the protocol decrees. "Parties to this declaration should not make any public announcement of this information" until the signal's extraterrestrial origin is verified.

"The world has changed a lot since the 1980s," says Franck Marchis, a senior planetary astronomer at the SETI Institute and an outreach and education coordinator for A Sign in Space. For one, there are many more radio aficionados like Carracedo Carballal who have rigged their own telescopes and trained them toward the skies. There's also social media, which spreads news like wildfire. "The public will know no matter what," Marchis says.

A Sign in Space is a dress rehearsal for scientific organizations to iron out the technical challenges of message sharing and telescope mobilization to confirm signal detection. More idealistically, it's an experiment for sharing an extraterrestrial signal with members of the public and getting them involved. In that sense, A Sign in Space is the ultimate citizen science project, one on a planetary scale. De Paulis calls the participants on Discord her "co-creators."

Marchis says he would love to make extraterrestrial communication and translation a more democratic affair. "I'd make the data available right away to the entire community of the world," Marchis says, rather than having it "on the internal network of some random scientists." That's what drew him to A Sign in Space in the first place. "I'm hoping that this is going to be the way we're going to move forward in the future," he says.

Many members of the public would be more than happy to get involved in the real deal, but they aren't holding their breath. "So many cool theories [on] this server," Hasanaj mused on Discord. The SETI Institute "should ask us to build the next message."

Science Meets Art

In construing the meaning of an extraterrestrial dispatch, those who give it a go often try to anticipate what the message might be trying to say. The go-to answer is often science and math, given that these concepts hold up anywhere in the universe. The movie Contact posits that space aliens will hail us with numbers, throwing us a sequence of primes that look unnatural enough to make humans sit up and take notice.

But science and math won't tell the recipients anything about the senders themselves. "If all I find is that the extraterrestrials know quadratic equations, I'm going to be very disappointed," Vakoch says.

It's one thing to flag a different species' attention but another to converse meaningfully across the vast reaches of space. "I think an alien would send information that gives us an idea of who they are and the level of complexity that they have reached," Marchis says—something that may even give recipients a glimpse of the alien society and its evolution.

This is where art comes in. Art is a creator's self-expression and a cross-cultural conversation with its beholder. Perhaps the true meaning of an alien's message is the composer's original intent plus what the recipients make of it. Parsing such a message requires not only technical skill but also an artistic, philosophical flex. Thus, communicating with aliens is both a science and an art.

A Sign in Space recognizes the near futility of extraterrestrial communication and turns it into an endeavor that's much more open-ended. "If we ever receive a message from an extraterrestrial civilization, I can imagine that there will never be an agreement over the cultural interpretation," de Paulis says. "I think there would necessarily be some miscommunication."

Understandably, the communication barrier can occasionally lead to griping. "It feels like interpreting clouds," wrote one user on Discord. "Am I going crazy?" Humans sometimes forget that everyday communication with one another is also a miracle in itself. In response to a string of posts in French, one user, who failed to recognize the irony, replied, "Please speak English." Moderators jumped in to say that all languages were welcome, which was followed by the French nonspeaker's swift apology.

About the Author

Shi En Kim is a science writer based in Washington, D.C. Her work has appeared in Chemical & Engineering News, National Geographic, Hakai Magazine, Slate, Science News, and more. Follow her on X (formerly Twitter) @goes_by_kim.

Is E.T. Eavesdropping on Our Phone Calls?

By Phil Plait

Ever worry about shadowy forces tapping your phone calls and listening in on your private conversations? Well, astronomers have some good news for you: it won't be aliens with their ears (or whatever auditory sensory organs they have evolved) to the speaker getting into your business—unless they've done a lot better than we have at funding radio astronomers. And even then, they'd have to be *really* close by.

Scientists working on SETI—the search for extraterrestrial intelligence—have long pondered how to detect life outside Earth. Assuming there are technologically advanced aliens out there, they might be trying to communicate with us, or they might just be leaking radio energy into the cosmos by accident. Either way, can we pick up that signal? One way to tackle this question is to turn it around: We know how much energy *we're* broadcasting into space. Given our own level of technology, could we detect such a signal from light-years away? If so, then maybe we can hear extraterrestrials, too.

SETI scientists have focused their efforts mostly on radio waves because they're easy to make; any young technological civilization will figure that out pretty quickly—after all, we did. They can be beamed with a lot of power, have lots of information encoded in them, and can travel easily through the myriad dust and gas clouds littering our local space environment. They're ideal for cross-galactic communication.

This kind of study has been done in the past; research published in the journal *Science* in 1978 looked at our television signals and military radar, the most powerful transmissions we could send into space. At that time radio telescopes could detect those emanations out to 25 and 250 light-years away, respectively. This is a volume of space that encompasses several hundred thousand stars. In the decades since, our broadcast TV signal has waned as we've turned to cable and the internet to deliver our shows. The days of wondering whether aliens loved *Lucy* as much as we did are behind us, I'm afraid.

But other communication methods are on the rise, and they could prove more fruitful for any aliens looking for another lonely civilization with which to chat. Research by SETI scientists published in the *Monthly Notices of the Royal Astronomical Society* looks at how our cell-phone usage might be detectable from other stars.

Without going into too much technical detail, cell phones emit a weak signal that can be detected by a nearby tower, which in turn emits a much stronger signal to send the transmission along. Coverage for a given phone company is divided into small areas called cells, each populated with one or perhaps a few towers that can pick up nearby phone signals.

The signal strength of an individual phone is only a fraction of a watt, but a tower emits a couple of hundred watts—about the same as a bright lightbulb. That's not much, but there are a lot of them. OpenCelliD, an open database of cell locations, has tens of millions of cells listed globally. The total power emitted by cell-phone transmissions can be measured in gigawatts.

What an alien would detect when pointing a radio telescope at Earth depends on more than just the combined signal strength of all those towers, though. The direction the towers transmit in is also important. Most human cell-phone users are located near Earth's surface, so the tower antennae are configured to send their signals parallel to the ground, covering it like lawn sprinklers spraying water. If you're on the ground near a tower, you'll get a strong signal from it, but if you're above it, you'll get at best a weak signal.

Tower locations matter as well. There are very few towers in the Pacific Ocean nations, compared with a huge number in the U.S. And there are more towers in the Northern Hemisphere than the Southern, so our alien friends would see a different signal depending on where their home star is located in the sky.

Putting this together, the scientists modeled what aliens would see from hypothetical planets orbiting three nearby stars: HD 95735, Barnard's Star, and Alpha Centauri A. All of these are less than nine light-years away, practically in our galactic backyard, maximizing the snooping capabilities of any nosy aliens. The stars are also widely spread in declination (the measure of latitude on the sky), meaning observers in those spots would see how Earth appears from different directions.

The conclusion? If the alien tech is the same as ours—with a radio telescope as big as the 100-meter Green Bank Telescope in West Virginia—our overall cell-phone signal is still far too weak to be detected from any of the three stars. The next-generation Square Kilometer Array, currently under construction in Australia and South Africa, will be more sensitive but still will have only about 1 percent of the sensitivity needed to detect Earth's transmissions from tens of trillions of kilometers away.

If aliens are anything like us, then, we're safe from eavesdropping. Judging from my time spent in airports and other public places, however, a lot of people don't care at all who overhears their calls. I wouldn't go so far as to say I hope aliens abduct them, but I'm not not saying that.

What if our galactic neighbors are more advanced technologically? Telescopes detecting interstellar radiation are like buckets set outside in a rain shower: the bigger the bucket, the more water it collects. It's technically feasible to build far larger radio telescopes than we have now. There are even serious proposals to build huge radio telescopes on the moon. These would be far more sensitive than what we have today, perhaps capable of picking up transmissions such as our mobile signals even from interstellar distances.

So there's still a chance that extraterrestrials could listen in on our cell-phone conversations, provided they are close enough, are in the right part of the sky, and have slightly better tech on hand (or tentacle or pseudopod) than we do now. You can decide which part of that last sentence is the most far-fetched, but in any case, that's a lot of ifs. The longest odds are that they're sufficiently close to us; if their home world is 1,000 light-years away, they'll need a telescope the size of a moon to pick up our transmissions. Possible, but a lot of effort.

Still, the scientists note that the number of terrestrial cell-phone towers is increasing, and we get brighter in radio emissions every day. They also plan on expanding their work to include more powerful 5G towers, radar, satellite services, and more to get a better handle on just how loudly we're announcing our presence in the galaxy. Remember, too, that all of this is to solve the more pertinent puzzle of whether we can hear them. That remains a maybe, an ambiguous and somewhat maddening conclusion. And of course, everything depends on the answer to the biggest question of all: Are they even out there?

If so, E.T., please phone Earth; we're eagerly awaiting your call.

About the Author

Phil Plait is a professional astronomer and science communicator in Virginia. He writes the Bad Astronomy *Newsletter. Follow him online.*

Want to Talk to Aliens? Try Changing the Technological Channel beyond Radio

By Adam Mann

The endeavor known as the search for extraterrestrial intelligence (SETI) has long relied on radio telescopes to listen for broadcasts from potential alien callers. Yet in an expansive galaxy such as ours, how can we ever be sure that we have tuned in to the right station?

A model simulating contact across the Milky Way suggests—perhaps unsurprisingly—that unless our galaxy is dense with long-lived intelligent species, the odds of stumbling across a signal are low. Yet the findings, which were published in 2020 in the *International Journal of Astrobiology*, also point out that the probability of interaction could be greatest at the moment when a novel communication technology first comes online.

Along with providing fodder for imaginative scenarios—we flip the switch on some new listening device and, *voilà*, receive a transmission from E.T.—the results might encourage would-be alien hunters to innovate. Research efforts dedicated to discovering and developing new methods to communicate across cosmic distances may ultimately offer greater chances of making contact than long programs that use a single technology.

For Marcelo Lares, the research began with a challenge. An astronomer at the National University of Córdoba in Argentina, Lares ordinarily works on data-rich statistical analyses involving stellar populations, the large-scale structure of the universe, and gravitational-wave events.

Thinking about aliens offers no such informational abundance. "We have just one observation, which is that Earth is the only known planet with life," Lares says.

Scientific speculations about otherworldly life, intelligence, and technology often rely on the Drake equation. This mathematical framework was first written down by astronomer Frank Drake in

1961. It estimates the number of communicating species by looking at the fraction of stars in the galaxy with planets, the percentage of those planets that develop life, and the odds that such living creatures will grow curious about, and capable of, making interstellar contact with other beings.

Lares and his collaborators wanted something simpler. Rather than hazarding guesses about the unknowns involved in life's genesis and the development of intelligence and technology, they created a model that had essentially three parameters: the moment when communicating species "awaken" and begin broadcasting evidence of their presence, the reach of such signals, and the lifetime of any given transmission.

The resulting arrangement places a bunch of nodes—or intelligent message creators—at random throughout the Milky Way, where they sometimes broadcast and sometimes do not. "It's like a Christmas tree," says astronomer José Funes of Catholic University of Córdoba, one of Lares's co-authors. "You have lights going on and off."

The team ran more than 150,000 simulations, each time with a different set of assumptions about these basic parameters, to see which scenarios favored interstellar contact. A galaxy full of technological aliens announcing themselves produced far more interactions than one where species were separated by vast distances or great amounts of time.

Such conclusions might not necessarily be shocking. "It's just a statistical way of saying, 'If you want to increase your chances of contact, you need greater numbers [of communicators] or have them last a long time,'" says planetary scientist Ravi Kopparapu of the NASA Goddard Space Flight Center, who was not involved in the work.

But Lares counters that quantifying our intuitive conceptions with mathematical models can be valuable, if only to serve as a reality check on our basic understanding. The findings set a kind of upper limit on the probability of contact under different circumstances, he adds.

In each case, the simulations showed that the odds of interstellar interaction are by far the largest just at the moment when a species "awakens" and figures out the right way to communicate. That result happens because other nodes will have already come online and presumably found one another, essentially creating a large branch of "lit up" Christmas tree lights and increasing the chances of stumbling across this broadcasting network. But if the lights are flashing out of sync with one another or at vastly different times—a situation that is analogous to using the wrong contact technology or being separated by large time spans—intelligent species might never find one another.

After SETI's historically preferred contact technology—radio waves—became commonly available in the early part of the 20th century, some discoveries were even initially thought to be alien transmissions. And in the 1960s British astronomers Jocelyn Bell Burnell and Antony Hewish originally called the first detection of a pulsar, a rapidly spinning stellar corpse, LGM-1 for "little green men" because the source's pulses seemed too regular to be natural. Yet humanity has slowly been sending out fewer radio emissions over the decades as we have upgraded our technology to wired and fiber-optic cables, which has lessened the chances that aliens might stumble across our leaking transmissions.

The study's authors see their findings as one possible answer to the Fermi paradox, which asks why we have not found evidence of intelligent aliens, given that in the long history of our galaxy, some technological species could have arisen and sent dispatches of its existence across space by now. The work suggests this absence is not very meaningful—perhaps E.T. is too far away from us in space and time or is just using some calling card that is unknown to us.

At the heart of the research is also an attempt to step away from some of the human-centric biases that tend to plague speculations about alien others. "It's very difficult to imagine extraterrestrial communication without our anthropomorphic way of thinking," Funes says. "We need to make an effort to exit from ourselves."

Kopparapu concurs with this assessment. "Unexpected discoveries come from unexpected sources," he says. "In our common-knowledge thinking, we are in a box. It is hard for us to accept that there could be something else outside it."

SETI's focus on radio waves developed under particular circumstances during a small slice of human history. Although the undertaking has sometimes tried other means to discover intelligent aliens, such as looking for high-powered laser beams or evidence of massive star-encircling artificial structures called Dyson spheres, any search still seemingly remains just as limited by the human imagination as it is by fundamental physics.

Yet looking for something as potentially fantastical as another cosmic culture requires the convergence of many disciplines, including physics, biology, and even philosophy, Lares says. The effort to consider more creative messages, such as ones made by neutrinos, gravitational waves or phenomena that science has yet to discover, can help break down our parochial conceptions and give us a fuller understanding of ourselves.

Despite the small odds of contact, Lares is hopeful that attacking the problem in many ways will one day pay off. "I think that a SETI search is a high-risk bet," he says. "The probability of success is actually very low. But the prize is really very high."

About the Author

Adam Mann is a journalist specializing in astronomy and physics. His work has appeared in National Geographic, the Wall Street Journal, Wired, *and elsewhere.*

Researchers Made a New Message for Extraterrestrials

By Daniel Oberhaus

U pon discovering the existence of intelligent life beyond Earth, the first question we are most likely to ask is "How can we communicate?" As we approach the 50th anniversary of the 1974 Arecibo message—humanity's first attempt to send out a missive capable of being understood by extraterrestrial intelligence—the question feels more urgent than ever. Advances in remote sensing technologies have revealed that the vast majority of stars in our galaxy host planets and that many of these exoplanets appear capable of hosting liquid water on their surface—a prerequisite for life as we know it. The odds that at least one of these billions of planets has produced intelligent life seem favorable enough to spend some time figuring out how to say "hello."

In early March an international team of researchers led by Jonathan Jiang of NASA's Jet Propulsion Laboratory posted a paper on the preprint server arXiv.org that detailed a new design for a message intended for extraterrestrial recipients. The 13-page epistle, referred to as the "Beacon in the Galaxy," is meant to be a basic introduction to mathematics, chemistry, and biology that draws heavily on the design of the Arecibo message and other past attempts at contacting extraterrestrials. The researchers included a detailed plan for the best time of year to broadcast the message and proposed a dense ring of stars near the center of our galaxy as a promising destination. Importantly, the transmission also features a freshly designed return address that will help any alien listeners pinpoint our location in the galaxy so they can—hopefully—kick off an interstellar conversation.

"The motivation for the design was to deliver the maximum amount of information about our society and the human species in the minimal amount of message," Jiang says. "With improvements in digital technology, we can do much better than the [Arecibo message] in 1974."

Message Basics

Every interstellar message must address two fundamental questions: what to say and how to say it. Nearly all the messages that humans have broadcast into space so far start by establishing common ground with a basic lesson in science and mathematics, two topics that are presumably familiar to both ourselves and extraterrestrials. If a civilization beyond our planet is capable of building a radio telescope to receive our message, it probably knows a thing or two about physics. A far messier question is how to encode these concepts into the communiqué. Human languages are out of the question for obvious reasons, but so are our numeral systems. Though the concept of numbers is nearly universal, the way we depict them as numerals is entirely arbitrary. This is why many attempts, including "Beacon in the Galaxy," opt to design their letter as a bitmap, a way to use binary code to create a pixelated image.

The bitmap design philosophy for interstellar communication stretches back to the Arecibo message. It is a logical approach—the on/off, present/absent nature of a binary seems like it would be recognized by any intelligent species. But the strategy is not without its shortcomings. When pioneering search for extraterrestrial intelligence (SETI) scientist Frank Drake designed a prototype of the Arecibo message, he sent the binary message by post to some colleagues, including several Nobel laureates. None of them were able to understand its contents, and only one figured out that the binary was meant to be a bitmap. If some of the smartest humans struggle to understand this form of encoding a message, it seems unlikely that an extraterrestrial would fare any better. Furthermore, it is not even clear that space aliens will be able to see the images contained within the message if they do receive it.

"One of the key ideas is that, because vision has evolved independently many times on Earth, that means aliens will have it, too," says Douglas Vakoch, president of METI (Messaging Extraterrestrial Intelligence) International, a nonprofit devoted to researching how to communicate with other life-forms. "But that's a big 'if,' and even if they can see, there is so much culture embedded in the way we represent objects. Does that mean we should rule out pictures? Absolutely not. It means we should not naively assume that our representations are going to be intelligible."

In 2017 Vakoch and his colleagues sent the first interstellar message transmitting scientific information since 2003 to a nearby star. It, too, was coded in binary, but it eschewed bitmaps for a message design that explored the concepts of time and radio waves by referring back to the radio wave carrying the message. Jiang and his colleagues chose another path. They based much of their design on the 2003 Cosmic Call broadcast from the Yevpatoriaradio telescope in the region of Crimea. This message featured a custom bitmap "alphabet" created by physicists Yvan Dutil and Stéphane Dumas as a protoalien language that was designed to be robust against transmission errors.

After an initial transmission of a prime number to mark the message as artificial, Jiang's message uses the same alien alphabet to introduce our base-10 numeral system and basic mathematics. With this foundation in place, the message uses the spin-flip transition of a hydrogen atom to explain the idea of time and mark when the transmission was sent from Earth, introduce common elements from the periodic table, and reveal the structure and chemistry of DNA. The final pages are probably the most interesting to extraterrestrials but also the least likely to be understood because they assume that the recipient represents objects in the same way that humans do. These pages feature a sketch of a male and female human, a map of Earth's surface, a diagram of our solar system, the radio frequency that the extraterrestrials should use to respond to the message, and the coordinates of our solar system in the galaxy referenced to the location of globular clusters—stable and tightly packed groups of thousands of stars that would likely be familiar to an extraterrestrial anywhere in the galaxy.

"We know the location of more than 50 globularclusters," Jiang says. "If there's an advanced civilization, we bet that, if they know astrophysics, they know the globular cluster locations as well, so we can use this as a coordinate to pinpoint the location of our solar system."

To Send or Not?

Jiang and his colleagues propose sending their message from either the Allen Telescope Array in northern California or the Five-Hundred-Meter Aperture Spherical Radio Telescope (FAST) in China. Since the recent destruction of the Arecibo telescope in Puerto Rico, these two radio telescopes are the only ones in the world that are actively courting SETI researchers. At the moment, though, both telescopes are only capable of listening to the cosmos, not talking to it. Jiang acknowledges that outfitting either telescope with the equipment required to transmit the message will not be trivial. But doing so is possible, and he says he and his co-authors are discussing ways to work with researchers at FAST to make it happen.*

If Jiang and his colleagues get a chance to transmit their message, they calculated that it would be best to do so sometime in March or October, when Earth is at a 90-degree angle between the sun and its target at the center of the Milky Way. This would maximize the chance that the missive would not get lost in the background noise of our host star. But a far deeper question is whether we should be sending a message at all.

Messaging extraterrestrials has always occupied a controversial position in the broader SETI community, which is mostly focused on listening for alien transmissions rather than sending out our own. To detractors of "active SETI," the practice is a waste of time at best and an existentially dangerous gamble at worst. There are billions of targets to choose from, and the odds that we send a message to the right planet at the right time are dismally low. Plus, we have no idea who may be listening. What if we give our address to an alien species that lives on a diet of bipedal hominins?

"I don't live in fear of an invading horde, but other people do. And just because I don't share their fear doesn't make their concerns irrelevant," says Sheri Wells-Jensen, an associate professor of English at Bowling Green State University and an expert on the linguistic and cultural issues associated with interstellar message design. "Just because it would be difficult to achieve global consensus on what to send or whether we should send doesn't mean we shouldn't do it. It is our responsibility to struggle with this and include as many people as possible."

Despite the pitfalls, many insist that the potential rewards of active SETI far outweigh the risks. First contact would be one of the most momentous occasions in the history of our species, the argument goes, and if we just wait around for someone to call us, it may never happen. As for the risk of annihilation by a malevolent space alien: We blew our cover long ago. Any extraterrestrial capable of traveling to Earth would be more than capable of detecting evidence of life in the chemical signatures of our atmosphere or the electromagnetic radiation that has been leaking from our radios, televisions, and radar systems for the past century. "This is an invitation to all people on Earth to participate in a discussion about sending out this message," Jiang says. "We hope, by publishing this paper, we can encourage people to think about this."

About the Author

Daniel Oberhaus is a science writer based in Brooklyn, N.Y. He was previously a staff writer at Wired *covering space exploration and the future of energy. His first book,* Extraterrestrial Languages *(MIT Press, 2019), is about the art and science of interstellar communication. Follow Oberhaus on X (formerly Twitter) @DMOberhaus.*

Can "Conversations" with Whales Teach Us to Talk with Aliens?

By Avery Schuyler Nunn

F or some scientists who are eager to talk with aliens, the best avenue isn't any telescope pointed to the heavens but rather a boat slipping through the glassy waters of Alaska's Frederick Sound. This area is a seasonal hotspot for humpback whales, whose eerie and enchanting submarine songs may serve as proxies for any alien transmissions that practitioners of SETI (the search for extraterrestrial intelligence) may eventually receive. In a recent paper published in the journal *Aquatic Biology*, a group of researchers reported a humpback encounter at Frederick Sound that they say is a compelling case of interspecies communication, with lessons for parsing future messages from the stars. But critics aren't so sure.

The debate highlights a lingering tension between SETI's lofty aspirations and the down-to-earth limits of our knowledge: How can we hope to find intelligent life out there—let alone chat with it—when we struggle to perceive and communicate with intelligent nonhuman creatures right here on our home world?

Laurance Doyle, an astronomer at the SETI Institute and a co-author of the study, says such questions are exactly why he and his colleagues were listening to whales in the first place. "We're trying to get on the outside of nonhuman intelligence," he says. "We're trying to understand it so that when we get an extraterrestrial signal, we'll know what to do."

The encounter occurred on August 19, 2021, around the 18-meter research vessel *Glacier Seal*. It began when Doyle and others onboard spotted a nearby humpback, which was later identified as a female nicknamed "Twain." Attempting to catch Twain's attention, the researchers used an underwater speaker to play a series of humpback vocalizations they had recorded in Frederick Sound in the prior afternoon. After three broadcasts reverberated through the depths, the creature slowly approached the boat. With every vocalization that echoed from the speaker, Twain responded in kind—often with a nearly identical call. For 20 minutes, the whale circled the *Glacier Seal*, engaging in the call-and-response exchange and making a total of 36 calls before swimming away—and leaving Doyle and his shipmates with the impression that they had just witnessed a potential milestone in human-cetacean communications.

One World, Many Minds

Notions of similar milestones trace back to SETI's very roots. At a historic meeting in 1961, a select group of scientists codified key tenets of the then-nascent field. One of the invited attendees was John Lilly, a neuroscientist who claimed to have talked with captive bottlenose dolphins at a specialized research center that he'd established in the U.S. Virgin Islands. Impressed by Lilly's research and his contributions to the meeting, the other participants ultimately called themselves the Order of the Dolphin. Although Lilly's controversial practices eventually pushed him far beyond the bounds of orthodox science, reputable researchers still acknowledge the importance of his early results, which laid the groundwork for more rigorous subsequent attempts at cetacean communication.

But then and now some fundamental stumbling blocks exist: How exactly should we quantify concepts like "communication" and "intelligence" across species? And can we do so in a way that minimizes our decidedly anthropocentric biases? For Doyle and the study's lead author, Brenda McCowan, an animal behaviorist at the University of California, Davis, one possible answer lies within the presumptive universal language of mathematics, filtered through analytic techniques from a subdiscipline known as information theory. "We have millions of communication systems on Earth—plants, animals, and so on," Doyle says. "But how communicative are they? The next question requires information theory."

Birthed in the late 1940s from the work of mathematician and computer scientist Claude Shannon, information theory underpins all modern digital communications. For instance, its methods for quantifying complexity and syntax are crucial for finding signals obscured by noise, as well as for making—and breaking—cryptographic codes. Presumably, then, information theory should be useful for deciphering and cataloging the information that is carried within not only whale songs and dolphin whistles but the signaling behaviors of many other organisms as well. This could, the thinking goes, eventually lead to transformative results—such as a hierarchical library of sorts, in which the diverse communication systems of Earth's biosphere are classified based on their complexity, whether found in humans, whales, plants, microbes, or any other living thing. That, in turn, could help form a framework for understanding different forms of intelligence, both on and beyond our isolated planet.

This objective and similarly audacious goals remain very much a work in progress. For now, researchers such as Doyle and McCowan are focused on simpler applications. In their encounter with Twain, they looked for a communication pattern called latency matching, deliberately shifting the timing between their broadcasts in hopes that the whale would match the temporal delays. That the whale did exactly this, they say, was in large part what made the interaction so compelling and noteworthy. Twain's latency matching, they speculate, may have been an attempt to engage in a discussion.

A Promising First Step

Yet many researchers—and even the study's authors themselves—are hesitant to say the exchange can be considered anything close to a "conversation."

Peter Tyack, a marine biologist at the University of St. Andrews in Scotland, who specializes in cetacean research and was not part of the study, is one such skeptic. Based on other latency-matching work dating back to the 1980s, he says, scientists have long known that whales—and many animals, for that matter—adjust the timing of their calls to avoid overlaps with another caller. So mere expediency, rather than curiosity, can adequately explain Twain's behavior. "I do not think that similar results from the authors' playbacks of humpback sound supports the claim that the whale was intentionally trying to create a cross-species interaction," he says.

Such criticisms—which assume that the whale didn't realize she was communicating with humans or at least couldn't discern that the sound wasn't emanating directly from another nearby whale— strike the study authors as special pleading. It's far more likely, they argue, that Twain knew the boat—if not its human passengers— was the proximate source of what she heard. "I think initially she could've thought it was her own sound or another whale, but she had these periods of time where she could have gone underwater to inspect us," says Fred Sharpe, a co-author of the study and a marine biologist at the Alaska Whale Foundation. Twain, he notes, stayed within 100 meters of the boat for the duration of the encounter, presumably reducing the chance of mistaken identity. And when the team ceased its broadcast because of protocol-mandated limits on their scientific study, he adds, Twain lingered for a time and kept calling—as if awaiting another response.

Outside of the debate about latency matching, other researchers who were not involved with the study are quick to suggest that its appeal may arise more from the charisma of its cetacean subjects rather than the notability of its science. After all, other animals—Alex the parrot, Koko the gorilla, and many less famous creatures—have shown evidence of symbolic communication and abstract thought in various investigations across the decades.

"This type of playback has been done many times with birds and frogs and in a much more rigorous context," notes behavioral ecologist and animal acoustic communication specialist Mickey Pardo of Cornell University, who wasn't involved in the new study. "A lot of other animals are highly intelligent but don't get as much credit as whales, and it hasn't been considered a 'conversation' in the past when we look at studies with other animals."

Pardo suggests that the team's encounter with Twain is best seen as a promising first step toward more ambitious future studies—ones in which researchers could attempt more interactive playback, test more honed hypotheses and incorporate participation from a larger number of whales.

"This is very preliminary, and we were very limited in the ways in which we could modify the signal," McCowan acknowledges. "It was such a rare and opportunistic circumstance with a being that is incredibly difficult to study, that we thought it should be shared. The idea is to go back and replicate something like this," she says.

Regardless of any extraterrestrial implications, there is hope that the study will contribute to conservation initiatives and the ways in which we engage with animals. Doyle notes that while the "head" of the research is its connection with SETI, its "heart" lies in reshaping our relationship with life here on Earth, to identify and—if possible—reduce our anthropocentric prejudices. "Maybe we need to think about animals differently on this planet. They themselves can be quite alien to us in many ways," McCowan says. "There's an analogy to be made here of equity, inclusion, and diversity of cultures both in our own species and across species—which is something we need to preach better to."

Earth's ocean and the whales that send their songs reverberating through its abyss offer analogies too—to the vast depths of outer space and the possibilities of beings somehow sending messages across light-years to commune with one another. In both cases, perhaps our struggle to find anyone to talk to is mostly a function of our ignorance, our failure to look and listen in the proper ways.

"If we're not picking up on animal intelligence, [their] overtures, or even deciphering their communication systems, no wonder we gaze out on a silent universe!" Sharpe says. "We could be awash with alien signals, and we just don't have the perceptual bandwidth yet or the ability to recognize and interpret them. A humpback whale illustrates that really well."

About the Author

Avery Schuyler Nunn is an avid surfer, free diver and environmental science journalist based in California. She earned her Master of Science degree from Columbia University in 2021 and has used her notebook and camera as tools for exploration, both above and beneath the surface, ever since. She is a freelance contributor to Scientific American, National Geographic, Smithsonian Magazine, Grist, *and more. Follow her work on Instagram and X (formerly Twitter) @earthyave and at www.averyschuylernunn.com.*

When Will We Hear from Extraterrestrials?

By Avi Loeb

W e have been carelessly leaking radio waves into space for 126 years without thinking about the consequences. If there is a neighboring civilization with sensitive radio telescopes within a hundred light years, they might already know about us. How quickly should we expect them to make contact?

There are two types of responses that we could anticipate. The faster would involve electromagnetic signals such as radio waves, which move at the speed of light. But this would mean waiting until the 22nd century for a civilization located even as close as 100 light years away. A much slower response would involve chemically propelled rockets, like *Voyager 1* and *2* or *New Horizons,* which our civilization has sent on trajectories that are taking them out into interstellar space. If the responders chose to use those, that "short" journey of 100 light-years would take millions of years. This means that we still would have a waiting time as long as the time that elapsed since humans first appeared on Earth before we could witness chemically propelled crafts arriving in response to detecting our TV and radio broadcasts. The travel time could be shortened considerably with extraterrestrial sails pushed by light up to relativistic speeds, in the spirit of the Starshot concept, but it would still take an enormous amount of time.

But that assumes that an extraterrestrial civilization is at the same stage of technological development as we are, but the Copernican principle, which asserts that we aren't special in any way, says otherwise. We have had the technology capable of reaching out to other stars for only about a century, just a tiny fraction of our Earth's history; the odds are more than 10 million to one that another planet is at precisely the same point in its own development. In order to encounter one, we would have to include a volume of space containing more than 10 million stars. Given the local density of stars, this implies that the signal must traverse a distance of at least a thousand light years. And that in turn requires a two-way light-travel time of more than two millennia. In other words, we will not get a response, even at light speed, before the year 4000.

There is another way to look at it, however. This was the conclusion of a paper that we recently submitted for publication with my student, Amir Siraj. We asked: What if an advanced technological civilization arose many millions of years ago and has been traveling across interstellar space since long before becoming aware of our existence? Our own astronomers are eager to study potentially habitable exoplanets, such as a planet around the nearest star, Proxima Centauri. We easily might decide to visit Proxima Centauri b with our spacecraft before there is any sign that a technological civilization might have emerged on it. In an analogous way, could interstellar vehicles be surprisingly close to us right now simply because their creators discovered long ago that Earth is a habitable planet and decided to come for a look?

The only way to find out is to search the sky for unusual objects. This is the rationale behind the Galileo Project, co-founded with my colleague Frank Laukien, which I am leading. The project was publicly announced on July 26, 2021, as a research endeavor to assemble and transparently analyze scientific data collected by new telescopes. This multimillion-dollar project is funded by private donors who approached me after reading my book *Extraterrestrial* or listening to the numerous interviews that followed its publication. Subsequently, I assembled an exceptional research team that plans to construct a network of new telescopes and monitor the sky for any unusual objects near Earth. When searching the sky in a new way, one is likely to discover something new.

This was true of the astronomer Galileo Galilei (1564–1642), whose improved design of an optical telescope allowed him to discover the four largest moons of Jupiter in 1609–1610. These Galilean moons were the first satellites found to orbit a planet other than Earth. Galileo also discovered Saturn's rings in 1610.

Both discoveries provided key evidence in favor of the model of heliocentrism, developed by Nicolaus Copernicus and published in 1543, which displaced the previous, dogmatic and incorrect, geocentric model of the universe. According to a popular legend, after recanting under persecution his theory that the Earth moved around the sun, Galileo allegedly muttered the rebellious phrase "And yet it moves." Galileo also complained that some of the philosophers who opposed his discoveries had refused even to look through his telescope and see the mountains on the moon or the four largest moons of Jupiter. Let us not repeat their mistake. Admitting that our knowledge is incomplete would allow us to complete our knowledge.

Our project is named after Galileo in view of the possibility that it could make pathbreaking discoveries regarding extraterrestrial technological civilizations. A high-resolution image of an extraterrestrial artifact could impact our world view as much as Galileo's pioneering observations.

This is an opinion and analysis article; the views expressed by the author or authors are not necessarily those of Scientific American.

About the Author

Avi Loeb is former chair (2011-2020) of the astronomy department at Harvard University, founding director of Harvard's Black Hole Initiative and director of the Institute for Theory and Computation at the Harvard-Smithsonian Center for Astrophysics. He also chairs the Board on Physics and Astronomy of the National Academies and the advisory board for the Breakthrough Starshot project, and is a member of President's Council of Advisors on Science and Technology. Loeb is the bestselling author of Extraterrestrial: The First Sign of Intelligent Life Beyond Earth *(Houghton Mifflin Harcourt).*

Section 4: Technology and the Search for Life

To Find Life in the Universe, Find the Computation

By Caleb A. Scharf

What if the search for life in the universe is really a search for how the cosmos computes? That's the intriguing, and perhaps unsettling, possibility that we are exploring as a part of our quest to find out whether or not we are alone.

Since the beginnings of our scientific understanding of genetic inheritance in the 1800s and our discovery of molecules like DNA and RNA in the 1900s, we've seen that life is informational in nature. There is a "code" of sorts at the heart of living things. It's a hugely complex code for sure, a code that constantly rewrites itself on the fly and isn't structured like our digital inventions, but we see it running across the wet, carbon-based biochemistry that pervades the Earth. And just like the manufacture and use of your power-hungry PC or game console, that biosphere reworks the planet, making it a Gaian machine of water and oxygen, nitrogen, and carbon.

That planetary reworking is something we might look for with telescopes like JWST, but it's a scientific struggle to fit all the pieces together to know what a planet and its life can become together. Critical questions revolve around how climate and geophysics provide an environment that can support life, and how life gets its energy and its essential chemical ingredients, and what it does with those.

Seeing biology as information might offer some answers. Independently, since the 1940s and the work of scientists like Claude Shannon, we've learned that information theory and the physics of thermodynamics are, in essence, one and the same way to describe the world. Information is always represented in matter—by 1s and 0s, or by one molecular bond or another—and information can in turn change matter's configurations. But it takes energy to make change, and so information and energy are endlessly swapping back and forth, all described by the laws of thermodynamics.

Pull these threads together, and life begins to look like information controlling matter to propagate. And that happens through processes that we would call computation—the shuffling and combination and recombination of information through algorithms that are themselves written in that same information. It's a mind-blowing, weed-smoking trip to contemplate. It also provides an extraordinary way to connect life and its habitats.

One of information thermodynamics' most important theoretical insights, drawing on 1950s work by John von Neumann and proposed by Rolf Landauer in 1961, is that there's an absolute energy cost to irreversibly changing any bit of information, something that you can never beat. That so-called Landauer limit is thanks to entropy (and the fact that organized change pushes again a universal tendency for disorder), and depends solely on the temperature at which the information change takes place.

Remarkably it seems that biology also adheres to that limit, and can operate very, very close to it. In 2017 the biologist and complexity scientist Chris Kempes and his colleagues pointed out that when the process of RNA translation takes an amino acid and attaches it to a chain of other amino acids (making or "computing" a protein inside cells) the energy involved is within a factor of 10 of the Landauer limit—which is an absolutely tiny 10-20 joules at room temperature.

What these findings hint at is a way to rewrite how we look for life, by instead looking for the "computational zones" of the universe, whether in RNA translation or in digital 1s and 0s or something else altogether. This is what I and my colleague and artificial life expert Olaf Witkowski have recently explored. If computation is universally constrained by the Landauer limit, which depends on temperature, as well as by how much energy and matter can be given over to computing, we can begin to chart out the prospects for computation on planets and elsewhere.

Computational zones can also upend conventional thinking on life's possibilities, or "habitable zones." If there's energy flow in an environment and matter to build with, we can say something about computation's potential, whether it's in rich hydrocarbon slush on Titan's frigid shorelines or molecules bouncing between the flowing cloud layers of Venus. Perhaps even in the subatomic constituents of a neutron star or the dispersed organic molecules of an entire galaxy's interstellar gases.

But we also have to figure out what parts of a living system are truly computational. DNA transcription or RNA translation look and smell like computation, and they're explicitly informational in nature. But what about metabolic processes, or gene regulation? This is where we have to be cautious in seeing terrestrial biology as any kind of "simple" collection of computational proesses. Learning life's complex informational hierarchies and functions is likely key to learning how life is implemented across the universe, where the same principles might have very different outcomes.

Searching for computational zones also dissolves the boundaries between what we think of as biology and technology. At the technological extremes are hypothetical concepts like Dyson structures that would capture all of a star's energy. If these structures are for computation, then we can figure out the design options afforded by thermodynamic and informational principles. Calculations hint that abundant substellar objects—so-called brown dwarfs, weighing in at a few percent the mass of our sun and a hundred thousand times less luminous—might be better Dyson energy sources for uncomplaining technology, but not for biology with its bothersome requirements for warmth and nutrients.

Perhaps though most of the universe's computation takes place somewhere between "pure" biology and pure technology. Humans are an example of a biology whose external machine structures now take on, and create, much of its computational needs. We're already a blended system, and that could be the most common type of life across the cosmos, and the type of life we're most likely to eventually detect.

It may also be the case that blended living systems are the only ones *able* to discover other living systems. Anything else will simply be incapable of noticing, or uninterested in what it shares the cosmos with. If that is true, we really do exist at the most exciting time for any species that has ever arisen on the Earth.

This is an opinion and analysis article, and the views expressed by the author or authors are not necessarily those of Scientific American.

About the Author

Caleb A. Scharf is a researcher and writer. He is the senior scientist for astrobiology at NASA's Ames Research Center in Silicon Valley.

Most Aliens May Be Artificial Intelligence, Not Life as We Know It

By Martin Rees and Mario Livio

T he Fermi paradox takes its name from a 1950s visit by physicist Enrico Fermi to the Los Alamos National Laboratory in New Mexico. One day, as Fermi was walking to lunch with physicist colleagues Emil Konopinski, Edward Teller, and Herbert York, one mentioned a *New Yorker* cartoon depicting aliens stealing public trash cans from the streets of New York. While dining later, Fermi suddenly returned to the topic of aliens by asking: "Where is everybody?"

Whereas not everybody agrees as to what Fermi was precisely questioning, the "paradox" has generally been interpreted as Fermi expressing his surprise over the absence of any signs for the existence of other intelligent civilizations in the Milky Way. Because a simple estimate showed that an advanced civilization could have reached every corner of the galaxy within a time much shorter than the galaxy's age, the question arose: Why don't we see them?

Over the years that have passed since Fermi asked his question, dozens of potential solutions to the "paradox" have been suggested.

In particular, a few scientists have argued that the absence of alien signals is the result of a "great filter"—an evolutionary bottleneck impenetrable to most life. If true, this great filter is either in our past or in our future. If it's behind us, then it may have occurred when life spontaneously emerged, for example, or when single-cell organisms transitioned to multicellular ones. Either way, it implies that complex life is rare, and we may even be alone in the Milky Way. If, on the other hand, the great filter is ahead of us, then most advanced civilizations may eventually hit a wall and cease to exist. If so, that too may be humanity's fate.

Instead, we would like to propose a new way of thinking about the Fermi paradox. It stands to reason that there are chemical and metabolic limits to the size and processing power of organic brains. In fact, we may be close to those limits already. But no such limits constrain electronic computers (still less, perhaps, quantum computers). So, by any definition of "thinking," the capacity and intensity of organic, human-type brains will eventually be utterly swamped by the cerebrations of artificial intelligence (AI). We may be near the end of Darwinian evolution, whereas the evolution of technological intelligent beings is only at its infancy.

Few doubt that machines will gradually surpass or enhance more and more of our distinctively human capabilities. The only question is when. Computer scientist Ray Kurzweil and a few other futurists think that AI dominance will arrive in just a few decades. Others envisage centuries. Either way, however, the timescales involved in technological advances span but an instant compared to the evolutionary timescales that have produced humanity. What's more, the technological timescales are less than a millionth of the vast expanses of cosmic time lying ahead. So, the outcomes of future technological evolution could surpass humans by as much as we intellectually surpass a comb jelly.

But what about consciousness?

Philosophers and computer scientists debate whether consciousness is a special property associated only with the kind of wet, organic brains possessed by humans, apes, and dogs. In other words, might electronic intelligences, even if their capabilities seem superhuman, still lack self-awareness or an inner life? Or perhaps consciousness emerges in any sufficiently complex network?

Some say that this question is irrelevant and semantic—like asking whether submarines swim. We don't think so. The answer crucially affects how we react to the far-future scenario we've sketched: If the machines are what philosophers refer to as "zombies," we would not accord their experiences the same value as ours, and the posthuman future would seem rather bleak. If, on the other hand, they are conscious, we should surely welcome the prospect of their future hegemony.

Suppose now that there are indeed many other planets on which life began, and that some or most followed a somewhat similar evolutionary track as Earth. Even then, however, it's highly unlikely that the key stages in that evolution would be synchronized with those on Earth. If the emergence of intelligence and technology on an exoplanet lags significantly behind what has happened on Earth (either because the planet is younger, or because some "filters" have taken longer to negotiate) then that planet would plainly reveal no evidence of an intelligent species. On the other hand, around a star older than the sun, life could have had a significant head start of a billion years or more.

Organic creatures need a planetary surface environment for the chemical reactions leading to the origin of life to take place, but if posthumans make the transition to fully electronic intelligences, they won't need liquid water or an atmosphere. They may even prefer zero gravity, especially for building massive artifacts. So it may be in deep space, not on a planetary surface, that nonbiological "brains" may develop powers that humans can't even imagine.

The history of human technological civilization may measure only in millennia (at most), and it may be only one or two more centuries before humans are overtaken or transcended by inorganic intelligence, which might then persist, continuing to evolve on a faster-than-Darwinian timescale, for billions of years. That is, organic human-level intelligence may be, generically, just a brief phase, before the machines take over. If alien intelligence has evolved similarly, we'd be most unlikely to catch it in the brief sliver of time when it was still embodied in the organic form. Particularly, were we to detect ET, it would be far more likely to be electronic, where the dominant creatures aren't flesh and blood—and maybe aren't even located on planets, but on stations in deep space.

The question then becomes whether the fact that electronic civilizations can live for billions of years seriously exacerbates the Fermi paradox. The answer is: not really. While most of us who are puzzled by the Fermi paradox and the absence of alien signs imagine other civilizations as being expansionist and aggressive, this is not necessarily the case. The key point is that whereas Darwinian natural selection has put in some sense at least a premium on survival of the fittest, posthuman evolution, which will not involve natural selection, need not be aggressive or expansionist at all. These electronic progeny of flesh and blood civilizations could last for a billion years—maybe leading quiet, contemplative lives.

The focus of the search for extraterrestrial intelligence (SETI) so far has been on radio or optical signals, but we should be alert also to evidence for non-natural construction projects, such as a "Dyson sphere," built to harvest a large fraction of stellar power, and even to the possibility of alien artifacts lurking within our solar system.

If SETI were to succeed, we think that it would be unlikely that the signal it observes would be a simple, decodable message. It would more likely be a byproduct (or maybe even an accident or malfunction) of some supercomplex machine far beyond our comprehension. Even if messages were transmitted, we may not recognize them as artificial because we may not know how to decode them. A veteran radio engineer familiar only with amplitude-modulation might have a hard time decoding modern wireless communication. Indeed, compression techniques today aim to make signals as close to noise as possible.

So to conclude: conjectures about advanced or intelligent life are on a far shakier ground than those about simple life. We would argue that this suggests three things about the entities that SETI searches could reveal:

They will not be organic or biological.

They will not remain on the surface of the planet where their biological precursors lived.

We will not be able to fathom their motives or intentions.

This is an opinion and analysis article, and the views expressed by the author or authors are not necessarily those of Scientific American.

About the Authors

Martin Rees is the 15th Astronomer Royal, and was master of Trinity College from 2004 to 2012 and president of the Royal Society between 2005 and 2010. He is also the author of 10 popular science books including On the Future.

Mario Livio worked for 24 years with the Hubble Space Telescope and is a fellow of the American Association for the Advancement of Science. Livio is also author of seven popular science books, including, most recently, Galileo and the Science Deniers *(Simon & Schuster, 2020).*

How Many Aliens Are in the Milky Way? Astronomers Turn to Statistics for Answers

By Anil Ananthaswamy

I n the 12th episode of *Cosmos*, which aired on December 14, 1980, the program's co-creator and host Carl Sagan introduced television viewers to astronomer Frank Drake's eponymous equation. Using it, he calculated the potential number of advanced civilizations in the Milky Way that could contact us using the extraterrestrial equivalent of our modern radio-communications technology. Sagan's estimate ranged from "a pitiful few" to millions. "If civilizations do not always destroy themselves shortly after discovering radio astronomy, then the sky may be softly humming with messages from the stars," Sagan intoned in his inimitable way.

Sagan was pessimistic about civilizations being able to survive their own technological "adolescence"—the transitional period when a culture's development of, say, nuclear power, bioengineering, or a myriad of other powerful capabilities could easily lead to self-annihilation. In essentially all other ways, he was an optimist about the prospects for pangalactic life and intelligence. But the scientific basis for his beliefs was shaky at best. Sagan and others suspected the emergence of life on clement worlds must be a cosmic inevitability, because geologic evidence suggested it arose shockingly quickly on Earth: in excess of four billion years ago, practically as soon as our planet had sufficiently cooled from its fiery formation. And if, just as on our world, life on other planets emerged quickly and evolved to become ever more complex over time, perhaps intelligence and technology, too, could be common throughout the universe.

In recent years, however, some skeptical astronomers have tried to put more empirical heft behind such pronouncements using a sophisticated form of analysis called Bayesian statistics. They have focused on two great unknowns: the odds of life arising on Earth-like planets from abiotic conditions—a process called abiogenesis—and, from there, the odds of intelligence emerging. Even with such estimates in hand, astronomers disagree about what they mean for life elsewhere in the cosmos. That lack of consensus is because even the best Bayesian analysis can only do so much when hard evidence for extraterrestrial life and intelligence is thin on the ground.

The Drake equation, which the astronomer introduced in 1961, calculates the number of civilizations in our galaxy that can transmit—or receive—interstellar messages via radio waves. It relies on multiplying a number of factors, each of which quantifies some aspect of our knowledge about our galaxy, planets, life, and intelligence. These factors include f_p, the fraction of stars with extrasolar planets; n_e, the number of habitable planets in an extrasolar system; f_l, the fraction of habitable planets on which life emerges; and so on.

"At the time Drake wrote [the equation] down—or even 25 years ago—almost any of those factors could have been the ones that make life very rare," says Ed Turner, an astrophysicist at Princeton University. Now we know that worlds around stars are the norm, and that those similar to Earth in the most basic terms of size, mass, and insolation are common as well. In short, there appears to be no shortage of galactic real estate that life could occupy. Yet "one of the biggest uncertainties in the whole chain of factors is the probability that life would ever get started—that you would make that leap from chemistry to life, even given suitable conditions," Turner says.

Ignoring this uncertainty can lead astronomers to make rather bold claims. For example, last month Tom Westby and Christopher Conselice, both at the University of Nottingham in England, made headlines when they calculated that there should be at least 36 intelligent civilizations in our galaxy capable of communicating with us. The estimate was based on an assumption that intelligent life emerges on other habitable Earth-like planets about 4.5 billion to 5.5 billion years after their formation.

"That's just a very specific and strong assumption," says astronomer David Kipping of Columbia University. "I don't see any evidence that that's a safe bet to be making."

Answering questions about the likelihood of abiogenesis and the emergence of intelligence is difficult because scientists just have a single piece of information: life on Earth. "We don't even really have one full data point," Kipping says. "We don't know when life emerged, for instance, on the Earth. Even that is subject to uncertainty."

Yet another problem with making assumptions based on what we locally observe is so-called selection bias. Imagine buying lottery tickets and hitting the jackpot on your 100th attempt. Reasonably, you might then assign a 1 percent probability to winning the lottery. This incorrect conclusion is, of course, a selection bias that arises if you poll only the winners and none of the failures (that is, the tens of millions of people who purchased tickets but never won the lottery). When it comes to calculating the odds of abiogenesis, "we don't have access to the failures," Kipping says. "So this is why we're in a very challenging position when it comes to this problem."

Enter Bayesian analysis. The technique uses Bayes's theorem, named after Thomas Bayes, an 18th-century English statistician and minister. To calculate the odds of some event, such as abiogenesis, occurring, astronomers first come up with a likely probability distribution of it—a best guess, if you will. For example, one can assume that abiogenesis is as likely between 100 million to 200 million years after Earth formed as it is between 200 million to 300 million years after that time or any other 100-million-year-chunk of our planet's history. Such assumptions are called Bayesian priors, and they are made explicit. Then the statisticians collect data or evidence. Finally, they combine the prior and the evidence to calculate what is called a posterior probability. In the case of abiogenesis, that probability would be the odds of the emergence of life on an Earth-like planet, given our prior assumptions and evidence. The posterior is not a single number but rather a probability distribution that quantifies any uncertainty. It may show, for instance, that abiogenesis becomes more or less likely with time rather than having a uniform probability distribution suggested by the prior.

In 2012 Turner and his colleague David Spiegel, then at the Institute for Advanced Study in Princeton, N.J., were the first to rigorously apply Bayesian analysis to abiogenesis. In their approach, life on an Earth-like planet around a sunlike star does not emerge until some minimum number of years, t_{min}, after that world's formation. If life does not arise before some maximum time, t_{max}, then, as its star ages (and eventually dies), conditions on the planet become too hostile for abiogenesis to ever occur. Between t_{min} and t_{max}, Turner and Spiegel's intent was to calculate the probability of abiogenesis.

The researchers worked with a few different prior distributions for this probability. They also assumed that intelligence took some fixed amount of time to appear after abiogenesis.

Given such assumptions, the geophysical and paleontological evidence of life's genesis on Earth and what evolutionary theory says about the emergence of intelligent life, Turner and Spiegel were able to calculate different posterior probability distributions for abiogenesis. Although the evidence that life appeared early on Earth may indeed suggest abiogenesis is fairly easy, the posteriors did not place any lower bound on the probability. The calculation "doesn't rule out very low probabilities, which is really sort of common sense with statistics of one," Turner says. Despite life's rapid emergence on Earth, abiogenesis could nonetheless be an extremely rare process.

Turner and Spiegel's effort was the "first really serious Bayesian attack on this problem," Kipping says. "I think what was appealing is that they broke this default, naive interpretation of the early emergence of life."

Even so, Kipping thought the researchers' work was not without its weaknesses, and he has now sought to correct it with a more elaborate Bayesian analysis of his own. For instance, Kipping questions the assumption that intelligence emerged at some fixed time after abiogenesis. This prior, he says, could be another instance of selection bias—a notion influenced by the evolutionary pathway by which our own intelligence emerged. "In the spirit of encoding all of your ignorance, why not just admit that you don't know that number either?" Kipping says. "If you're trying to infer how long it takes life to emerge, then why not just also do intelligence at the same time?"

That suggestion is exactly what Kipping attempted, estimating both the probability of abiogenesis and the emergence of intelligence. For a prior, he chose something called the Jeffreys prior, which was designed by another English statistician and astronomer, Harold Jeffreys. It is said to be maximally uninformative. Because the Jeffreys prior doesn't bake in massive assumptions, it places more weigh on the evidence. Turner and Spiegel had also tried to find an uninformative prior. "If you want to know what the data is telling you and not what you thought about it previously, then you want an uninformative prior," Turner says. In their 2012 analysis, the researchers employed three priors, one of which was the least informative, but they fell short of using Jeffreys prior, despite being aware of it.

In Kipping's calculation, that prior focused attention on what he calls the "four corners" of the parameter space: life is common, and intelligence is common; life is common, and intelligence is rare; life is rare, and intelligence is common; and life is rare, and intelligence is rare. All four corners were equally likely before the Bayesian analysis began.

Turner agrees that using the Jeffreys prior is a significant advance. "It's the best way that we have, really, to just ask what the data is trying to tell you," he says.

Combining the Jeffreys prior with the sparse evidence of the emergence and intelligence of life on Earth, Kipping obtained a posterior probability distribution, which allowed him to calculate new odds for the four corners. He found, for instance, that the "life is common, and intelligence is rare" scenario is nine times more likely than both life and intelligence being rare. And even if intelligence is not rare, the life-is-common scenario has a minimum odds ratio of 9 to 1. Those odds are not the kind that one would bet the house on, Kipping says. "You could easily lose the bet."

Still, that calculation is "a positive sign that life should be out there," he says. "It is, at least, a suggestive hint that life is not a difficult process."

Not all Bayesian statisticians would agree. Turner, for one, interprets the results differently. Yes, Kipping's analysis suggests that life's apparent early arrival on Earth favors a model in which abiogenesis is common, with a specific odds ratio of 9:1. But this calculation does not mean that model is nine times more likely to be true than the one that says abiogenesis is rare, Turner says, adding that Kipping's interpretation is "a little bit overly optimistic."

According to Turner, who applauds Kipping's work, even the most sophisticated Bayesian analysis will still leave room for the rarity of both life and intelligence in the universe. "What we know about life on Earth doesn't rule out those possibilities," he says.

And it is not just Bayesian statisticians who may have a beef with Kipping's interpretation. Anyone interested in questions about the origin of life would be skeptical about claimed answers, given that any such analysis is beholden to geologic, geophysical, paleontological, archaeological, and biological evidence for life on Earth—none of which is unequivocal about the time lines for abiogenesis and the appearance of intelligence.

"We still struggle to define what we mean by a living system," says Caleb Scharf, an astronomer and astrobiologist at Columbia. "It is a slippery beast, in terms of scientific definition. That's problematic for making a statement [about] when abiogenesis happens—or even statements about the evolution of intelligence."

If we did have rigorous definitions, problems persist. "We don't know whether or not life started up, stopped, restarted. We also don't know whether life can only be constructed one way or not," Scharf says. When did Earth become hospitable to life? And when it did, were the first molecules of this "life" amino acids, RNAs or lipid membranes? And after life first came about, was it snuffed out by some cataclysmic event early in Earth's history, only to restart in a potentially different manner? "There's an awful lot of uncertainty," Scharf says.

All this sketchy evidence makes even Bayesian analysis difficult. But as a technique, it remains the best–suited method for handling more evidence—say, the discovery of signs of life existing on Mars in the past or within one of Jupiter's ice-covered, ocean-bearing moons at the present.

"The moment we have another data point to play with, assuming that happens, [the Bayesian models] are the ways to best utilize that extra data. Suddenly, the uncertainties shrink dramatically," Scharf says. "We don't necessarily have to survey every star in our galaxy to figure out how likely it is for any given place to harbor life. One or two more data points, and suddenly, we know about, essentially, the universe in terms of its propensity for producing life or possibly intelligence. And that's rather powerful."

About the Author

Anil Ananthaswamy is author of The Edge of Physics *(Houghton Mifflin Harcourt, 2010),* The Man Who Wasn't There *(Dutton, 2015), and, most recently,* Through Two Doors at Once: The Elegant Experiment That Captures the Enigma of Our Quantum Reality *(Dutton, 2018).*

New Instrument Could Spy Signs of Alien Life in Glowing Rocks

By Allison Gasparini

W as Mars ever a living world? Billions of years ago, before it became a freeze-dried desert, the Red Planet was much more Earth-like, with liquid water and clement temperatures at its surface. Perhaps it harbored life, too. But most signs of any ancient Martians would by now be little more than traces of organic compounds and faint fossil forms hidden in the planet's rusted rocks.

Scientists today use robots to survey that barren landscape, remotely guiding their search for life through a combination of satellite pictures and on-the-ground snapshots from the rovers and landers themselves. Such imagery, however, leaves much to be desired—for all but the very closest views, rocks devoid of biosignatures versus ones teeming with fossilized microorganisms may be almost indistinguishable. Now, in a study recently published in *Scientific Reports*, a team led by researchers at the University of Hawaii has shown a possible shortcut for finding the most promising targets for astrobiological follow-up, whether on the Red Planet or some other world elsewhere in the solar system.

The technique relies on a curious fact of biology—earthly biology, anyway: Across life's many kingdoms, all sorts of organisms produce pigments, proteins, lipids, and other molecules that emit a telltale glow—fluorescence—when they are excited by certain wavelengths of light. Using carefully tuned laser pulses on fossil-bearing multimillion-year-old rocks from Colorado, Wyoming, and Utah's Green River Formation, the researchers demonstrated such "biofluorescence" can be an effective way to rapidly, efficiently flag candidate biological material for more detailed scrutiny. Their prototype instrument, dubbed the Compact Color Biofinder, is sensitive enough to detect the presence of biofluorescent materials from up to five meters away, even in daylight, and can project the laser pulses across a wide target area, allowing sizable swaths of territory to be rapidly surveyed.

That unique daytime sensitivity, team members say, makes the decade-in-development Biofinder an especially attractive option for seeking out remnants of ancient life. The capability comes from the instrument's camera, which captures brief exposures of targets. "When you have a camera that opens for a short time, then you actually don't detect the daylight," explains Anupam Misra, a researcher at the University of Hawaii and lead author on the paper.

Another notable strength of the instrument is its—so to speak—agnostic attitude toward life detection. Whereas other laboratories searching for extraterrestrial life may target the most detailed components of life as it appears on Earth—such as certain sequences of DNA common among single-celled organisms thriving in extreme environments on our planet—the Compact Color Biofinder takes a much more general approach. All it seeks are compounds that will fluoresce when stimulated by laser pulses. On Earth, all living organisms possess aromatic amino acids, usually as a by-product of metabolic processes. All aromatic amino acids display fluorescence. Given the ubiquity of fluorescent amino acids with life, the researchers assumed that even if life on other planets doesn't use the exact amino acids found on Earth, they can still detect it as long as it fluoresces. "If there's life on Mars and it's not 'life as we know it,' then the Biofinder may be the only way we see it," says study co-author Christopher McKay, an astrobiologist and planetary scientist at NASA's Ames Research Center.

One challenge is that amino acids and biological compounds aren't the only materials on Earth that emit light when stimulated by lasers. Abiotic minerals also emit their own light, called phosphorescence. It can be confused with biofluorescence, but the team built the Biofinder from the start to distinguish between these two very different phenomena. In general, phosphorescence signals are much longer-lasting than their fluorescent counterparts, allowing the Biofinder to distinguish between them.

Although McKay suggests the Biofinder could be the best bet for discovering ancient remnants of unknown life-forms on Mars, that's not to say the instrument would provide the final word in understanding what exactly it had caught on camera. "You can look at a pie, but tasting it gives you a lot more information about it," he says.

Any samples lit up by the Biofinder would then need to be "digested" in analytic instruments in laboratories for scientists to get a better understanding of what they found, McKay says. But where he finds the Biofinder's general nature to be a plus, Patrick Gasda, a researcher at Los Alamos National Laboratory, sees the lack of specifics as the approach's main downside. Gasda worked on SuperCam, an instrument onboard the Mars rover *Perseverance*. SuperCam sifts through the rock and soil on Mars using laser spectroscopy, bathing targets in highly focused beams of laser light to gather more specific information about the underlying chemical composition. "You could see if there's carbon and nitrogen," he says. But even spectroscopy isn't the same as a real digestive analysis. "You'd still probably want to take a sample of it" for more direct, rather than remote, study, he says.

Although he was not involved in the most recent study, Gasda worked on the Biofinder in 2012 while pursuing his Ph.D. as Misra's student at the University of Hawaii. Right now Gasda is working with Misra on a version of the Biofinder called the OrganiCam. Like the Biofinder, OrganiCam uses laser-induced fluorescence imaging to spot signs of life. But it adds a chemical analysis technique called Raman spectroscopy, which uses a laser to determine the molecular composition of the target. Also like the Biofinder, the OrganiCam is not yet spaceflight-ready. In addition to needing to be miniaturized to fit on a lander, Gasda says, both instruments also require more robust housings and microcircuitry to allow them to endure rocket launches, planetfall, and the deleterious effects of cosmic radiation.

Whereas the Biofinder may offer breakthrough applications for space exploration *someday*, it could be of more immediate use right here on Earth for seeking out life in extreme—and perhaps extremely delicate—environments. As an example, McKay cites caverns filled with giant gypsum crystals buried deep within a mountain range in Mexico. Exotic life-forms may comfortably exist within the crystals, he says—but the only way to check right now would be to hammer them open and look inside. "Sacrilege!" McKay says. "There's got to be a better way." With something like the Biofinder, researchers could instead subject such crystals to less invasive probes.

Whether on Earth, Mars, or some other world entirely, McKay says, "the core idea from my point of view is being able to understand the biology of a target without chipping or drilling or sampling."

About the Author

Allison Gasparini is a science writer who has written for Forbes, Science News, *NASA, Brookhaven National Laboratory, the American Institute of Physics, Stanford University, and more. Follow her on X (formerly Twitter) @astrogasparini.*

JWST Heralds a New Dawn for Exoplanet Science

By Jonathan O'Callaghan

Any future historian of 21st-century space science may well divide the subject into two eras: before the James Webb Space Telescope (JWST) and after. The telescope was built to transform our understanding of the cosmos by studying the first stars and galaxies, and within less than a year of operations, it has already delivered tantalizing and potentially revolutionary results from its observations of the early universe. Yet JWST's work is poised to transform many other subfields of astronomy, none arguably more so than the study of exoplanets, worlds orbiting other stars. Astronomers now know *of* more than 5,000 exoplanets but know next to nothing *about* most of them—their composition, environmental conditions, or even prospects for life. JWST is beginning to change that, thanks to its as-yet-unparalleled ability to directly observe these alien worlds, picking apart their light to discern finer details and occasionally even managing to snap an exoplanet's picture against the overwhelming glare of its home star.

Such results remain a far cry from the astrobiological holy grail of finding and studying potentially Earth-like worlds but are enormously exciting nonetheless, given that JWST and its core science goals were conceived before exoplanets were even known to exist. "The exoplanet community is just giddy at the moment," says Mark Clampin, director of the Astrophysics Division at NASA Headquarters in Washington, D.C.

JWST's first year of science is scheduled from July 2022 through June 2023. Of that period, called Cycle 1, about a quarter of the telescope's time is being devoted to exoplanets across about 75 programs. One of the most exciting applications of JWST is studying exoplanet atmospheres. Gold-plated and about as wide as a full-grown African elephant, the telescope's infrared-tuned primary mirror allows it to probe the atmospheres of exoplanets to a degree never before possible. "With the Hubble [Space Telescope], we've done a decade of detecting water, which we found abundantly, but not much else," says Nikole Lewis of Cornell University. "That was the only thing you could measure." JWST can see water, too—as well as a much wider array of molecules including carbon dioxide, sodium, and more. Some of the compounds JWST can detect, such as methane, are closely associated with metabolic processes in Earth's biosphere, making them possible biosignatures that could help reveal life's presence on other potentially habitable worlds beyond the solar system.

In August astronomers revealed they had used JWST to detect carbon dioxide on an exoplanet for the first time by watching for signs of the gas in the light of a gas giant planet's host star filtering through the world's atmosphere. Known as transmission spectroscopy, this technique is incredibly useful not only for studying giant planets but also for investigating smaller ones that might be more like our solar system's retinue of rocky worlds. "We needed to start with 'OK, do they have air?'" Lewis says. "Once we understand that, we can develop a better strategy of looking for biosignature gases."

At the 241st meeting of the American Astronomical Society (AAS) in Seattle earlier this month, astronomers announced another transmission spectroscopy result from JWST. This time the telescope studied an Earth-sized world called LHS 475 b, which orbits a red dwarf star 41 light-years away from Earth. In this case, JWST actually confirmed the planet's existence, which previously had been hinted at by NASA's Transiting Exoplanet Survey Satellite (TESS). "We confirmed it was a planet by observing it with JWST," says Sarah Moran of the University of Arizona, a collaborator on the result.

JWST observed two orbits of the planet around its star, but an additional observation expected in May will be needed to better parse the contents of the planet's atmosphere. So far, however, the team "can say a lot of things about what the atmosphere is not like," Moran says. "We know it's not hydrogen-dominated like Jupiter or Saturn. We think it probably does not have an Earth-like atmosphere. But it could have a carbon dioxide atmosphere like Venus or Mars, or it could have no atmosphere at all like Mercury." Those results could help inform the study of other rocky planets around red dwarfs, which account for some three quarters of all stars in the Milky Way. "We're in the very first stages of trying to measure atmospheres for rocky planets and trying to figure out if a planet can be habitable," Moran says.

In terms of studying rocky planets, JWST is largely limited to worlds that orbit red dwarfs, which are dim enough to avoid overloading the telescope's exquisitely sensitive optics. Such stars are known to be prone to intense flaring that could blast away the atmospheres of worlds like LHS 475 b, which orbit perilously close to their host stars in comparison with the much wider star-planet separations among our solar system's rocky worlds. "There's the possibility that absolutely all of their atmospheres have been blown away by their stars," Lewis says. One major red dwarf target of interest, the TRAPPIST-1 system nearly 40 light-years from Earth, contains seven Earth-sized worlds. Several of these are in the star's habitable zone—the region around the star in which sufficient planet-warming starlight might allow liquid water to exist. Early observations of TRAPPIST-1 are still underway, including ones seeking out atmospheres. Those results could go a long way toward revealing whether red dwarf worlds can actually be habitable. "Hopefully we'll know by the end of Cycle 1," Lewis says.

JWST also sports an exciting add-on called a coronagraph, a device for blocking most of the light of stars so that fainter accompanying planets can be seen (this was crucial for JWST's first-ever exoplanet image, which researchers unveiled last September). The starlight-suppressing power of the telescope's coronagraph is insufficient for revealing any small, potentially habitable worlds, but recent work has shown the coronagraph should allow JWST to see worlds down to the size of Jupiter or Saturn that are orbiting red dwarf stars at or beyond five times the Earth-sun distance (five astronomical units, or AU). That's roughly the position of Jupiter in our own solar system.

This analysis comes from Kellen Lawson of NASA's Goddard Space Flight Center and his colleagues, who at the recent AAS meeting debuted stunning infrared views of a sprawling debris disk encircling a young star some 32 light-years from Earth. "In the past, direct imaging has been limited to 10 or so Jupiter masses," Lawson says. "Here we're sensitive to a [single] Jupiter mass." That will allow JWST to look for rough analogues of Jupiter around other stars in a way not possible before. "Our hope is, with JWST, we can constrain the presence of planets in this regime," Lawson says. Such directly imaged planets can be directly pinpointed in their orbits around their stars, giving a prime opportunity "to follow-up and get a ton of really incredible data."

Astronomers are also excited about the exoplanet capabilities of another telescope, the European Space Agency's (ESA's) Gaia observatory. Launched to space in 2013 primarily to map the motions and positions of billions of stars in our galaxy, the telescope is also expected to find thousands of exoplanets. At the AAS meeting, Sasha Hinkley of the University of Exeter in England—who leads one of JWST's early exoplanet imaging programs—announced that, using Gaia and the Very Large Telescope (VLT) in Chile, his team had seen an unusual planet some 130 light years from Earth that appeared to be undergoing nuclear fusion. "It's burning deuterium," he says, referring to a hydrogen isotope that achieves starlight-powering nuclear fusion at lower temperatures than normal hydrogen. Further studies of the system, Hinkley says, could help astronomers draw less blurry lines among stars, planets, and brown dwarfs—the latter being a loosely defined class of objects that fall between planets and stars in mass. The 130-light-year-distant planet, spotted thanks to Gaia witnessing a wobble in its host star's motion caused by the unseen world's gravitational pull, could be one of many upcoming exoplanets found by the telescope, some of which could also be interesting targets for JWST.

The quest for Earthlike worlds, however, seems set to define JWST's exoplanet legacy despite being largely beyond the telescope's reach. "That's where all this work is headed," Hinkley says, "and that's why a majority of people are in this game." In 2026 a new ESA mission called PLATO will launch, with finding such worlds as its primary goal. PLATO will stare at vast swathes of the sky to, for the first time, hunt in earnest for Earth-like worlds around sunlike stars within about 1,000 light-years of the solar system. A few tens of such planets are expected to be found during the telescope's four-year primary mission, says Ana Heras of ESA, the mission's project scientist. "We really don't know what the occurrence rate is [for Earth-like planets]," she says. PLATO will go some way to telling us how many, if any, there are in our corner of the galaxy.

JWST will not be able to closely study such worlds. Nor will its successor, the Nancy Grace Roman Space Telescope, set to launch by 2027, be capable of doing so. But Roman will play a crucial role alongside its other scientific objectives: testing the advanced coronagraph technology that will be needed to produce images of potentially habitable Earth-like worlds around stars like our sun. That technology is meant to then be employed on JWST and Roman's successor, the newly dubbed Habitable Worlds Observatory, which is set to launch no sooner than the late 2030s on a mission to produce the first-ever images of potentially habitable Earths. That telescope must be "about 100 times more stable" in space than JWST to achieve such a goal, says Bruce Macintosh, director of the University of California Observatories. "That's not a negligible challenge."

The road to this eventuality is a long one. "We're at the beginning of a journey here," Clampin says. But even leaving aside any talk of holy grails, JWST's transformative early exoplanet results remain a thrill for scientists. The best, however, is still yet to come. "People need to be patient," Lewis says. "The first cycle is all about picking the low-hanging fruit. We're going to start going crazy in the next few cycles."

About the Author

Jonathan O'Callaghan is an award-winning freelance journalist covering astronomy, astrophysics, commercial spaceflight and space exploration. Follow him on X (formerly Twitter) @Astro_Jonny.

Section 5: A New Approach?

The Search for Extraterrestrial Life as We Don't Know It

By Sarah Scoles

S arah Stewart Johnson was a college sophomore when she first stood atop Hawaii's Mauna Kea volcano. Its dried lava surface was so different from the eroded, tree-draped mountains of her home state of Kentucky. Johnson wandered away from the other young researchers she was with and toward a distant ridge of the 13,800-foot summit. Looking down, she turned over a rock with the toe of her boot. To her surprise, a tiny fern lived underneath it, having sprouted from ash and cinder cones. "It felt like it stood for all of us, huddled under that rock, existing against the odds," Johnson says.

Her true epiphany, though, wasn't about the hardiness of life on Earth or the hardships of being human: It was about aliens. Even if a landscape seemed strange and harsh from a human perspective, other kinds of life might find it quite comfortable. The thought opened up the cosmic real estate, and the variety of life, she imagined might be beyond Earth's atmosphere. "It was on that trip that the idea of looking for life in the universe began to make sense to me," Johnson says.

Later, Johnson became a professional at looking. As an astronomy postdoc at Harvard University in the late 2000s and early 2010s she investigated how astronomers might use genetic sequencing—detecting and identifying DNA and RNA—to find evidence of aliens. Johnson found the work exciting (the future alien genome project!), but it also made her wonder: What if extraterrestrial life didn't have DNA or RNA or other nucleic acids? What if their cells got instructions in some other biochemical way?

As an outlet for heretical thoughts like this, Johnson started writing in a style too lyrical and philosophical for scientific journals. Her typed musings would later turn into the 2020 popular science book *The Sirens of Mars*. Inside its pages, she probed the idea that other planets were truly other, and so their inhabitants might be very different, at a fundamental and chemical level, from anything on this world. "Even places that seem familiar—like Mars, a place that we think we know intimately—can completely throw us for a loop," she says. "What if that's the case for life?"

If Johnson's musings are correct, the current focus of the hunt for aliens—searching for life as we know it—might not work for finding biology in the beyond. "There's this old maxim that if you lose your keys at night, the first place you look is under the lamppost," says Johnson, who is now an associate professor at Georgetown University. If you want to find life, look first at the only way you know life can exist: in places kind of like Earth, with chemistry kind of like Earthlings'.

Much of astrobiology research involves searching for chemical "biosignatures"—molecules or combinations of molecules that could indicate the presence of life. But because scientists can't reliably say that ET life should look, chemically, like Earth life, seeking those signatures could mean we miss beings that might be staring us in the face. "How do we move beyond that?" Johnson asks. "How do we contend with the truly alien?" Scientific methods, she thought, should be more open to varieties of life based on varied biochemistry: life as we don't know it. Or, in a new term coined here, "LAWDKI."

Now Johnson is getting a chance to figure out how, exactly, to contend with that unknown kind of life, as the principal investigator of a new NASA-funded initiative called the Laboratory for Agnostic Biosignatures (LAB). LAB's research doesn't count on ET having specific biochemistry at all, so it doesn't look for specific biosignatures. LAB aims to find more fundamental markers of biology, such as evidence of complexity—intricately arranged molecules that are unlikely to assemble themselves without some kind of biological forcing—and disequilibrium, such as unexpected concentrations of molecules on other planets or moons. These are proxies for life as no one knows it.

Maybe someday, if LAB has its way, they will become more than proxies. These signals could help answer one of humankind's oldest questions—Are we alone?—and show us that we're not so special, and neither is our makeup.

Life, Astro Life or Lyfe

Part of the difficulty in searching for life of any sort is that scientists don't agree on how life started in the first place—or what life even is. One good attempt at a definition came in 2011 from geneticist Edward Trifonov, who collated more than 100 interpretations of the word "life" and distilled them into one overarching idea: it's "self-reproduction with variations." NASA formulated a similar working definition years earlier, in the mid-1990s, and still uses it to design astrobiology studies. Life, according to this formulation, "is a self-sustaining chemical system capable of Darwinian evolution."

Neither of those classical definitions requires a particular chemistry. On Earth, of course, life runs on DNA: deoxyribonucleic acid. DNA is made up of two twisted strands, each comprising alternating sugar and phosphate groups. Stuck to every sugar is a base—the As (adenine), Gs (guanine), Cs (cytosine), and Ts (thymine). Together the bases and sugar-phosphates form nucleotides; DNA itself is a nucleic acid. RNA is kind of like single-stranded DNA—among other things, it helps translate DNA's instructions into actual protein production.

The simple letters in a genetic sequence, strung together in a laddered order, carry all the information needed to make you, squirrels and sea anemones. DNA can replicate, and DNA from different organisms (when they really, really love one another) can mix and meld to form a new organism that can replicate itself in turn. If biology elsewhere relied on this same chemistry, it would be life as we know it.

Scientists assume all forms of life would need some way to pass down biological instructions whose shifts could also help the species evolve over time. But it's conceivable that aliens might not make these instructions out of the same chemicals as ours—or in the same shape. For instance, starting in the 1990s, Northwestern University researchers made SNAs, spherical nucleic acids.

Alien life could have genetic code with, say, different bases. NASA-supported 2019 research, from the Foundation for Applied Molecular Evolution, successfully created synthetic DNA that used the four old-school bases and four new ones: P, Z, B, and S. Scientists have also altered the strand part of genetic code, creating XNA—where X means anything goes—that uses a molecule such as cyclohexene (CeNA) or glycol (GNA), rather than deoxyribose. Big thinkers have long suggested that rather than using carbon as a base, as all these molecules do, perhaps alien life might use the functionally similar element silicon—meaning it wouldn't have nucleic acids at all but other molecules that perhaps play the same role. If we can whip up such diversity in our minds and our labs, shouldn't the universe be even more creative and capable?

It's for that reason that LAB collaborator Leroy Cronin of the University of Glasgow doesn't think scientists should even be talking about *biology* off-Earth at all. "Biology is unique," he proclaims. RNA, DNA, proteins, typical amino acids? "Only going to be found on Earth." He thinks someday people will instead say, "We're looking for "astro life." (LAWDKI has yet to catch on.)

Stuart Bartlett, a researcher at the California Institute of Technology and unaffiliated with LAB, agrees with the linguistic critique. The search for weird life isn't actually a search for life, Bartlett argues. It's a search for "lyfe," a term proposed in a 2020 article he co-authored in, ironically, the journal *Life*. "Lyfe," the paper says, "is defined as any system that fulfills all four processes of the living state." That means that it dissipates energy (by, say, eating and digesting), uses self-sustaining chemical reactions to make exponentially more of itself, maintains its internal conditions as external conditions change, and takes in information about the environment that it then uses to survive. "Life," meanwhile, the paper continues, "is defined as the instance of lyfe that we are familiar with on Earth."

Bartlett's work, though separate from LAB's, emerges from the same fascination: "That mysterious, opaque transition between things like physics and chemistry that we understand fairly well," he says, "and then biology that is still shrouded in mystery." How life becomes life at all is perhaps the most central question of astrobiology.

Trying to figure out how biology emerged on the planet we know best is the province of "origin of life" studies. There are two main hypotheses for how clumps of chemistry became lumps of biology—a process called abiogenesis. One holds that RNA arose able to make more of itself, because that's what it does, and that it could also catalyze other chemical reactions. Over time that replication led to beings whose makeup relied on that genetic code. The "metabolism-first" framework, on the other hand, posits that chemical reactions organized in a self-sustaining way. Those compound communities and their chemical reactions grew more complex and eventually spit out genetic code.

Those two main hypotheses aren't mutually exclusive. John Sutherland, a chemist at the Medical Research Council Laboratory of Molecular Biology, is co-director of a group called the Simons Collaboration on the Origins of Life, which merges previous ideas about how one or another subsystem, such as genetics or early metabolism, came first. But if he's being real, Sutherland admits he doesn't understand how biology got started. No one does.

And until scientists know more about how things probably went down on the early Earth, Sutherland argues, there's no way to estimate how common extraterrestrial anything might be. It doesn't matter that there are trillions of stars in billions of galaxies: If the events that led to life are supremely uncommon, those many solar systems might still not be enough, statistically, to have resulted in abiogenesis—in other beings.

Bio-Agnostic

The first issue of the academic journal *Astrobiology*, more than two decades ago, featured an article by Kenneth Nealson and Pamela Conrad called "A Non-Earth-centric Approach to Life Detection." But taking a non-Earth-centric approach isn't easy for our brains, which formed in this environment. We are notoriously bad at picturing the unfamiliar. "It's one of the biggest challenges we have, like imagining a color we've never seen," Johnson says.

So astrobiologists often end up looking for aliens that resemble Earth life. Astronomers like to consider oxygen in an exoplanet atmosphere as a potential indicator of life—because we breathe it—although a planet can fill up with that gas in less lively ways. On Mars, researchers have been psyched by puffs of methane, organic molecules, and the release of gas after soil was fed a solution of what we on Earth call nutrients, perhaps indicating metabolism. They create terms like "the Goldilocks zone" for the regions around stars where planets could host liquid water, implying that what's just right for Earth life is also just right everywhere else.

Even when scientists do discover biology unfamiliar to them, they tend to relate it to something familiar. For instance, when Antonie van Leeuwenhoek saw single-celled organisms through his microscope's compound lens in the 17th century, he dubbed them "animalcules," or little animals, which they are not.

Heather Graham, who works at NASA's Goddard Space Flight Center and is LAB's deputy principal investigator, sees van Leeuwenhoek's discovery as a successful search for LAWDKI, close to home. The same description applies to scientists' discovery of Archaea, a domain of ancient single-celled organisms first recognized in the 1970s. "If you reframe those discoveries as agnostic biosignatures in action, you realize that people have been doing this for a while," Graham says.

Around 2016, Johnson joined their ranks, finding some like-minded nonbelievers who wanted to probe that darkness. At an invitation-only NASA workshop about biosignatures, Johnson sat at a table with scientists like Graham, gaming out how they might use complexity as a proxy for biology. On an exaggerated macroscale, the idea is that if you come across a fleet of 747s on Mars, you might not know where they came from, but you know they're unlikely to be random. Someone, or something, created them.

After the meeting, Johnson and her co-conspirators put in a last-minute proposal to develop an instrument for NASA. It would find and measure molecules whose shapes fit physically together like lock and key because that rarely happens in random collections of chemical compounds but pops up all over living cells. The instrument idea, though, didn't make the cut. "That's when we realized, 'Okay, we need to roll this back and do a lot more fundamental work,'" Graham says.

The space agency would give them a chance to do so, soon putting out a call for "Interdisciplinary Consortia for Astrobiology Research." It promised multiple years of funding to dig deeper into Johnson and her associates' lunch-table ideas. They needed a larger team, though, so they pinged planetary scientists, biologists, chemists, computer scientists, mathematicians, and engineers—some space-centric to the core and others, Johnson says, "just beginning to consider the astrobiology implications of their work." It was particularly important to do this now because researchers are planning to send life-detection instruments to destinations such as the solar system moons Europa, Enceladus, and Titan, more exotic than most of the worlds visited so far. "Most of these other places we're beginning to think about as targets for astrobiology are really weird and different," Johnson says. If you're going to a weird and different place, you might expect weird and different life, squirming invisibly beyond the reach of a lamppost's light.

Their pitch worked: The expanded lunch table became LAB. Now the project, a spread-out coalition of scientists more than a single physical laboratory, is a few years deep into its work. The researchers aim to learn how things like the complexity of a surface, anomalous concentrations of elements and energy transfer—such as the movement of electrons between atoms—might reveal life as no one knows it.

Lab Work

LAB's research is a combination of fieldwork, lab projects and computation. One project is a planned visit to Canada's Kidd Creek Mine, which drops nearly 10,000 feet into the ground. Its open pit looks like a quarry reaching toward the seventh circle of hell. At those depths, around 2.7 billion years ago, an ocean floor brewed with volcanic activity, which left sulfide ore behind. The conditions are similar(ish) to what astronomers believe they might find on an "ocean world" like Europa. In the mine, the scientists hope to probe the differences between minerals that formed by crystallization—when atoms fall out of solution and into an ordered, lattice structure in the same place they are now—and evidence of biology.

The two kinds of materials can look superficially alike because they're both highly ordered. But the team aims to show that geochemical models, which simulate how water saturated with chemicals will precipitate them out, will predict the kind of abiotic crystals found there. Kidd Creek, for instance, has its own sort: Kiddcreekite, a combination of the copper, tin, tungstenm and sulfur that crystallizes from the water. Those same models, however, aren't likely to predict biological structures, which form according to different forces and rules. If that turns out to be true, the models may prove useful when applied to alien geochemical conditions to predict the naturally forming minerals. Anything else that's found there, the thinking goes, might be alive.

Johnson is reaching back to her postdoc days, using the genetic sequencers whose relevance she called into question back then. The group, though, has found a way to make them more agnostic. The researchers plan to use the instruments to investigate the number of spots on a cell's surface where molecules can attach themselves—like the places where antibodies stick to cells. "We had this hypothesis that there are more binding sites on something complicated like a cell than a small particle," Johnson says, such as an unalive mote of dust. Something alive, in other words, should have more lock-and-key places.

To test this idea, they create a random pool of DNA snippets and send it toward a cell. Some snippets will hook up with the cell's exterior. The scientists next remove and collect the bound snippets, then capture the unbound snippets and send them back to the target cell again, repeating the process for several cycles. Then they see what's left at the end—how much has hooked on and how much is still free. In this way, the researchers can compare the keys locked into the cell with those attached to something like a dust particle.

The scientists will also scrutinize another key difference they suspect divides life and not-life: Things that are not alive tend to be at a kind of equilibrium with their environment. In contrast, something that's alive will harness energy to maintain a difference from its surroundings, LAB member Peter Girguis of Harvard hypothesizes. "It's using power to keep ourselves literally separate from the environment, defining our boundary," he says. Take this example: When a branch is part of a tree, it's alive, and it's different—in a bordered way—from its environment. If you remove that life from its energy source—pluck the branch—it dies and stops using power. "In a matter of time, it disintegrates and becomes indistinguishable from the environment," Girguis says. "In other words, it literally goes to equilibrium."

The disequilibrium of living should show up as a *chemical* difference between an organism and its surroundings—regardless of what the surroundings, or the life, are made of. "I can go scan something, make a map and say, 'Show me the distribution of potassium,'" Girguis says. If blobs of concentrated K appear, dotting the cartography only in certain spots, you may have biology on your hands.

Girguis's LAB work intertwines with another pillar of the group's research: a concept called chemical fractionation, which is how life preferentially uses some elements and isotopes and ignores others. A subgroup investigating this idea, led by Christopher House of Pennsylvania State University, can use the usual data that space instruments take to suss out the makeup of a planet or moon. "If you understand the fundamental rules about the inclusion or exclusion of elements and isotopes, then you can imagine a different ecosystem where it still behaves by similar rules, but the elements and isotopes are totally different," House says. It could give disequilibrium researchers a starting point for which kinds of patterns to focus on when making their dotted maps.

Within House's group, postdoc researchers are studying sediments left by ancient organisms in Western Australia. Looking at these rock samples, they try to capture patterns showing which elements or isotopes early Earth life was picky about. "We're hopeful that we can start to generalize," House says.

LAB's computing team, co-led by Chris Kempes of the Santa Fe Institute, is all about such generalizing. Kempes's research focuses on a concept called scaling—in this case, how the chemistry inside a cell changes predictably with its size and how the abundance of different-sized cells follows a particular pattern. With LAB, Kempes, House, Graham and their collaborators published a paper in 2021 in the *Bulletin of Mathematical Biology* about how scaling laws would apply to bacteria. For instance, if you sort a sample of biological material by size, differences pop out. Small cells' chemistry looks a lot like their environment's. "The bigger cells will be more and more different from the environment," Kempes says.

The abundance of cells of different sizes tends to follow a relationship known as a power law: Lots of small things with a steep drop-off as cells get larger. If you took an extraterrestrial sample, then, and saw those mathematical relationships play out—small things that looked like their surroundings, with progressively larger things looking less like their environments, with lots of the former and few of the latter—that might indicate a biological system. And you wouldn't need to know ahead of time what either "environment" or "biology" looked like chemically.

Cronin, a sort of heretic within this heretic group, has his own idea for differentiating between living and not. He's an originator of something called assembly theory, a "way of identifying if something is complex without knowing anything about its origin," he says. The more complex a molecule is, the more likely it is to have come from a living process.

That can sound like a bias in the agnosticism, but everyone generally concedes that life results from, as Sutherland puts it, "the complexification of matter." In the beginning, there was the big bang. Hydrogen, the simplest element, formed. Then came helium. Much later there were organic molecules—conglomerations of carbon atoms with other elements attached. Those organic molecules eventually came together to form a self-sustaining, self-replicating system. Eventually that system started to build the biological equivalent of 747s (and then actual 747s).

In assembly theory, the complexity of molecules can be quantified by their "molecular assembly number." It's just an integer indicating how many building blocks are required to bond together, and in what quantities, to make a molecule. The group uses the word "abracadabra" (magic!) as an example. To make that magic, you first need to add an *a* and a *b*. To that *ab*, you can add *r*. To *abr*, toss in another *a* to make *abra*. Then attach a *c*, then an *a* and then a *d*, and you get *abracad*. And to *abracad*, you can add the *abra* that you've already made. That's seven steps to make *abracadabra*, whose molecular assembly number is thus seven. The group postulated that a higher number meant a molecule would have a more complicated "fingerprint" on a mass spectrometer—a tool that separates a sample's components by their mass and charge to identify what it's made of. A complex molecule would show more distinct peaks of energy, in part because it was made of many bonds. And those peaks are a rough proxy for its assembly number.

Cronin had bragged that by doing mass spectrometry, he could measure the complexity of a molecule without even knowing what the molecule was. If the technique indicated that a molecule's complexity crossed a given threshold, it probably came from a biological process.

Still, he needed to prove it. Through LAB, NASA gave him double-blind samples of material to yea or nay as biological. The material hailed from outer space, fossil beds, and the sediments of bays, among other places. One of the samples was from the Murchison meteorite, a 220-pound hunk of rock, full of organic compounds. "They thought the technique would fail because Murchison is probably one of the most complex interstellar materials," he says. But it succeeded: "It basically says Murchison seems a bit weird, but it's dead."

Another sample contained 14-million-year-old fossils, sculpted by biology but meant to fool the method into a "dead" hit because of their age. "The technique found that they were of living origin pretty easily," Cronin says. His results appeared in *Nature Communications* in 2021 and helped to convince Cronin's colleagues that his line of research was worthy. "There are a lot of skeptical people in [LAB's] team, actually," he says.

Aliens Discovered??

There is plenty of skepticism outside LAB as well. Some scientists question the need to search for unfamiliar life when we still haven't done much searching for extraterrestrial life as we know it. "I think there's still a lot we can explore before we go to life as we don't know it," says Martina Preiner of the Royal Netherlands Institute for Sea Research and Utrecht University.

Still, even among old-school astrobiology researchers looking for Earth-like signatures on exoplanets, the LAB approach has support. Victoria Meadows of the University of Washington has been thinking about such far-off signals for two decades. She's seen the field change over that time—complexify, if you will. Scientists have gone from thinking "if you see oxygen on a planet, slam dunk," to thinking "there are no slam dunks." "I think what my team has helped provide and how the field has evolved is this understanding that biosignatures must be interpreted in the context of their environment," she says. You have to understand a planet's conditions, and those of its star, well enough to figure out what oxygen might *mean*. "It may be that the environment itself can either back up your idea that oxygen is due to life or potentially that the environment itself may produce a false positive," she says, such as from an ocean boiling off.

In a lot of ways, Meadows says, looking for agnostic biosignatures is the ultimate way to take such cosmic conditions into account. "You have to understand the environment exquisitely to be able to tell that something anomalous—something that isn't a planetary process—is operating in that environment," she says. Still, this variety of alien hunting is in its infancy. "I think they're really just starting off," she says. "I think what LAB is doing in particular is a pioneering effort on really getting some science under this concept."

Even so, Meadows isn't sure how likely LAWDKI is. "The question is, 'Is the environment on a [terrestrial] extrasolar planet going to be so different that the solutions are so different?'" Meadows asks. If the conditions are similar and the chemicals are similar, it's reasonable to think life itself will be similar. "We are expecting to see some similar science if these environments are similar, but of course I will expect that there'll be things that will surprise us as well." It's for all these reasons that Meadows, whose work focuses on exoplanets, is working with the LAB scientists, whose research for now homes in on the solar system, to bring their two worlds together.

By the end of LAB's grant, the team plans to develop instruments that will help spacecraft notice weird and different life close to home. "We're extremely focused on the ultimate goal—how we can take these tools and techniques and help develop them to the point they can become instruments on space missions," Johnson says.

No one piece of information, gathered from a single instrument, can reliably label something life, though. So the group is working toward suites of devices, drawing on all their focus areas, that work together in different environments, such as worlds wrapped in liquid versus rocky deserts. Graham is gathering sample sets that LAB's subgroups can test in a round-robin way to see how the superimposition of their results stacks up. They might look for, say, molecules with big assembly numbers concentrated in bounded areas that look different from their environment.

Even if these approaches collectively find something, it's unlikely to provide a definitive answer to the question "Are we alone?" It will probably yield a "maybe," at least for a while. That grayness may disappoint those who'd like "Aliens discovered!" headlines, instead of "Aliens discovered?? Check back in 10 years."

"I understand that frustration," Johnson says, "because I'm a restless sort of person." That restlessness relates in part to her own mortality. The end of the time when she's out of equilibrium with her environment. The demise of her complexity, of her detectability and ability to detect. "We have these ephemeral lives," she says. "We have this world that's going to end. We have this star that's going to die. We have this incredible moment. Here we are: alive and sentient beings on this planet." All because, at some point, life *started*.

That may have happened tens or hundreds or thousands or millions or billions of other times on other planets. Or, maybe, it has only happened here. "It just feels," Johnson says, "like an extraordinary thing that I want to know about the universe before I die."

About the Author

Sarah Scoles is a Colorado-based science journalist, a contributing editor at Scientific American *and* Popular Science, *and a senior contributor at* Undark. *She is author of* Making Contact *(2017) and* They Are Already Here *(2020), both published by Pegasus Books. Her newest book is* Countdown: The Blinding Future of Nuclear Weapons *(Bold Type Books, 2024).*

How to Search for Life as We Don't Know It

By Avi Loeb

I n my freshman seminar at Harvard University in spring 2021, I mentioned that the nearest star to the sun, Proxima Centauri, emits mostly infrared radiation and has a planet, Proxima b, in the habitable zone around it. As a challenge to the students, I asked: "Suppose there are creatures crawling on the surface of Proxima b. What would their infrared-sensitive eyes look like?" The brightest student in class responded within seconds with an image of the mantis shrimp, which possesses infrared vision. The shrimp's eyes look like two Ping Pong balls connected with cords to its head. "It looks like an alien," she whispered.

When trying to imagine something we've never seen, we often default to something we have seen. For that reason, in our search for extraterrestrial life, we are usually looking for life as we know it. But is there a path for expanding our imagination to life as we don't know it?

In physics, an analogous path was already established a century ago and turned out to be successful in many contexts. It involves conducting laboratory experiments that reveal the underlying laws of physics, which in turn apply to the entire universe. For example, around the same time the neutron was discovered in the lab of James Chadwick in 1932, Lev Landau suggested that there might be stars made of neutrons. Astronomers realized subsequently that there are, in fact, some 100 million neutron stars in our Milky Way galaxy alone—and a billion times more in the observable universe. Relatively recently, the LIGO experiment detected gravitational-wave signals from collisions between neutron stars at cosmological distances. It is now thought that such collisions produce the precious gold that is forged into wedding bands. The moral of this story is that physicists were able to imagine something new in the universe at large and search for it in the sky by following insights gained from lab experiments on Earth.

The search for extraterrestrial life can follow a similar approach. By creating synthetic life in various ways from a soup of chemicals in the lab, we might be able to imagine new environments where life might occur differently than on Earth. The situation is similar to composing a recipe book with prescriptions for baking different types of cakes. To write a rich recipe book, we need to experiment with many types of chemicals. And, as I noted in a paper with Manasvi Lingam, this experimentation may use fluids other than water, which is considered essential for life as we know it.

One of my Harvard colleagues, the Nobel laureate Jack Szostak, is getting close to creating synthetic life in his lab. Any success with a single recipe may suggest variations that would produce a diversity of outcomes, to be assembled into our recipe book for synthetic life. By identifying suitable environmental conditions from our lab experiments, we can later search for real systems where they are realized in the sky, just as in the case of neutron stars.

In following this approach, we should be as careful as we are in tapping nuclear energy. Creating artificial variants of life in our labs brings the risk of causing an environmental disaster, as imagined in the story of Frankenstein. Such experimentation must be performed in isolated environments so that mishaps with life as we don't know it will not endanger the life we know.

Although the surfaces of planets and asteroids can be explored remotely for biological signatures, extraterrestrial life might be most abundant under the surface. Habitable conditions could exist in the oceans that lie under thick icy surfaces, not only within moons such as Saturn's Enceladus and Jupiter's Europa but also inside free-floating objects in interstellar space. In other research with Lingam, we showed that the number of life-bearing objects could exceed the number of rocky planets in the habitable zone around stars by many orders of magnitude.

The adaptation of life to extreme environments could take exotic forms, as exemplified by extremophiles on Earth. For example, frozen microscopic animals were recently discovered to survive 24,000 years in the Siberian permafrost, and microbial life was found to persist 100 million years underneath the seafloor. These microbes were born during the warm Cretaceous period when dinosaurs dominated Earth.

In the solar system, the closest conditions to Earth's were realized on its nearest neighbors, Venus and Mars. NASA has selected two new missions to study Venus, and its *Perseverance* rover is searching for traces of life on Mars. If extraterrestrial life is found, the key follow-up question is whether it is life as we know it. If not, we will realize that there are multiple chemical pathways to natural life. But if we find evidence for Martian or Venusian life that resembles terrestrial life, then that might indicate a special preference for life as we know it. Alternatively, life could have been transported by rocks that traveled between planets through a process called panspermia. My student Amir Siraj and I wrote a paper showing that the transfer of life could have been mediated by planet-grazing asteroids. We should also keep in mind the very remote possibility that life was seeded in the inner solar system by an "extrasolar gardener," namely, through "directed panspermia."

My most vivid childhood memory is of dinner conversations in which the adults in the room pretended to know much more than they actually did. This was undoubtedly a form of "intellectual makeup" that they wore to improve their appearance. And if I asked a question to which these pretenders had no ready answer, they would dismiss it as irrelevant. My experience as a senior scientist is no different, especially when asking the question: "Are we the smartest kid on the cosmic block?"

Science offers the privilege of maintaining our childhood curiosity. The advance of scientific knowledge through experimentation cannot be stopped. Here's hoping that we will find a recipe for artificial life that will allow us to imagine something far more intelligent than the natural life we have encountered so far. This will be a humbling experience. But even if we do not discover this supreme intelligence in our labs, its by-products may just show up in our sky as mail posted from faraway neighborhoods in the Milky Way. And we'll be searching for that through the telescopes of our Galileo Project, launched in 2021."

This is an opinion and analysis article; the views expressed by the author or authors are not necessarily those of Scientific American.

About the Author

Avi Loeb is former chair (2011-2020) of the astronomy department at Harvard University, founding director of Harvard's Black Hole Initiative and director of the Institute for Theory and Computation at the Harvard-Smithsonian Center for Astrophysics. He also chairs the Board on Physics and Astronomy of the National Academies and the advisory board for the Breakthrough Starshot project, and is a member of President's Council of Advisors on Science and Technology. Loeb is the bestselling author of Extraterrestrial: The First Sign of Intelligent Life Beyond Earth *(Houghton Mifflin Harcourt).*

Cultural Bias Distorts the Search for Alien Life

By Camilo Garzón

S ince time immemorial, humans have looked to the heavens above to make sense of life below, right here on Earth. What else is out there among all the countless galaxies, stars, and planets? Are we truly alone in the universe? Such questions are crucial for establishing humanity's cosmic context and have inspired a variety of speculative answers from a wide range of philosophical and scientific traditions. Buddhists believe in different Buddhas living in different worlds. The Greek atomists also believed in the plurality of worlds. And as early as the 19th century, Western scientists postulated ways to detect and communicate with putative Martians on the Red Planet. In each case, preexisting cultural biases served to profoundly shape prevailing ideas about the nature of life beyond Earth.

Today, under the auspices of the search for extraterrestrial intelligence (SETI), astronomers seek out space aliens by using some of the world's most powerful telescopes to look for clearly artificial electromagnetic transmissions emanating from interstellar or even intergalactic sources. So far, no convincing evidence of otherworldly messages has been found. Perhaps that's simply because there isn't anyone else out there to talk to. But increasingly, SETI scientists are grappling with the disquieting notion that, much like their intellectual forebears, their search may somehow be undermined by biases they only dimly perceive—biases that could, for instance, be related to the misunderstanding and mistreatment of Indigenous peoples and other marginalized groups that occurred during the development of modern astronomy and many other scientific fields.

For years, science historian Rebecca Charbonneau has been exploring this possibility in the context of SETI. She earned her Ph.D. at the University of Cambridge studying the history of radio astronomy, and is currently a historian in residence at the Harvard-

Smithsonian Center for Astrophysics, as well as a Jansky Fellow at the National Radio Astronomy Observatory. Her most recent paper, "Imaginative Cosmos: The Impact of Colonial Heritage in Radio Astronomy and the Search for Extraterrestrial Intelligence," appeared last year in a special SETI-themed issue of the *American Indian Culture and Research Journal*. To weed out biases and enhance the quest to find life somewhere among the stars, she argues, SETI's practitioners must find a way to "decolonize" their field. But what exactly does that mean?

Scientific American spoke to Charbonneau about decolonization, SETI's feedback loop with its own context and history, and how combating cultural biases in the search for alien life can be a case study for similar reforms in other STEM fields.

[An edited transcript of the interview follows.]

Garzón: "Decolonization" seems to be a problematic term, in part because it carries so much historical baggage and is used in many different ways across many different fields. Finding consensus about what it actually means is challenging, to say the least. So, to start out, what does decolonization mean to you?

Charbonneau: It's something I think about a lot because it is a very difficult problem. Some of the major problems with the term "decolonization" is that it has been watered down to mean any kind of conversation about colonialism. That really weakens the term. There was a paper written by these two great scholars, Eve Tuck and K. Wayne Yang, called "Decolonization Is Not a Metaphor," where they make the argument that when we're talking about decolonizing, it shouldn't be about just speaking in metaphors. This is actually a real-world process that has to happen—actual, physical colonization which needs to be undone.

Garzón: How does this apply to SETI?

Charbonneau: Oftentimes when we think about colonialism in SETI, we do think of it primarily in metaphors, right? Space being "the final frontier," first contact with aliens as a stand-in for encounters with Indigenous peoples—that sort of thing. But it actually is much more than a metaphor. Because space exploration is also an extension of our imperial and colonial histories. We know that space infrastructure, including SETI infrastructure, exists in remote locations, with places that often have colonial histories or vulnerable populations, particularly Indigenous peoples. And then space, despite our best efforts, is highly militarized. Nations talk about becoming space superpowers, building new empires, and colonizing other planets. So it's not just a metaphor. It's actually happening *in* the world and *off* the world, and that's why I think it's a useful term when we're talking about SETI. And SETI in particular carries a lot of intellectual, colonial baggage as well, especially in its use of abstract concepts like "civilization" and "intelligence," concepts that have been used to enact real, physical harm on Earth.

Garzón: If decolonization isn't just a metaphor but rather a process, that implies it's about reckoning with history and striving to fix past mistakes. That's something easy to say but much harder to actually define, let alone to do. In the context of SETI, what might decolonization's "reckoning" look like?

Charbonneau: It's a great question. Ultimately, in Tuck and Yang's interpretation of decolonization, this would look like prioritizing the sovereignty of Indigenous cultures and respecting their wishes regarding settled scientific infrastructure. And while that is critically important, we shouldn't entirely discount the symbolic, dare I say metaphorical, nature of colonialism at play in SETI. Fundamentally, SETI concerns listening to alien civilizations, ideally, but we also have to get better at listening to Earthlings! We're not very good at that right now, but we're starting to move in that direction. There are members of the SETI community, myself included, who are very interested in listening to marginalized and historically excluded perspectives.

A lot of SETI scientists start their research from the technical search perspective, without deeply considering the implications and impact of their listening. They are simply interested in finding evidence of intelligent extraterrestrial civilizations, which is valuable. I think that to do that, however, without thinking critically about how we conceptualize big abstract ideas, such as "intelligence" and "civilization," and without considering the ethics of the search and its cultural implications, would be a huge mistake. These ideas are tightly bound with the histories of racism, genocide, and imperialism, and to use them haphazardly can be harmful. How we use these symbols of the past when thinking about alien civilizations also says a lot about how we view Earth's civilizations, and this is where Indigenous Studies scholars, such as those who contributed to the special SETI issue of the *American Indian Culture and Research Journal*, can make great contributions. They have a unique perspective on the impact of contact, and how concepts like "intelligence" can be weaponized.

Garzón: It does feel ironic. SETI is built around listening for something out there but perhaps at the cost of ignoring much of what is *right here* on this planet. For instance, you've repeatedly mentioned the cultural implications of terms such as "intelligence" and "civilization," but how about the word "alien," too? All of these terms have very different connotations—even destructive ones—as historically applied to Indigenous peoples or, for that matter, as applied to all the other sentient beings that live on Earth. Even now some people don't consider nonhuman animals to be sentient, let alone possessing any real intelligence. And throughout history, building empires has come at the cost of discounting and dehumanizing Indigenous peoples as lesser beings, incapable of sophisticated thought and societal organization. Yet "intelligence" is right there in SETI's name. Should we reconsider that framing?

Charbonneau: SETI is designed to listen outward, but as you said, it's not always so great at listening inward. And I should preface this by saying that there are members of the SETI community who are very interested in doing this work. And oftentimes these missteps are not made consciously—we're all operating within our own cultural frameworks. And so, of course, when we are thinking about the "other," the imagined alien, we're going to project our own understanding of what that looks like onto this blank slate. In fact, some people even call SETI a mirror. Jill Tarter, an eminent SETI scientist, famously referred to SETI as holding up a cosmic mirror, where we're looking for the "other," but in the process of doing that, we are really learning about ourselves.

As for "intelligence," that's certainly a dangerous word, and it has been used in very harmful ways. Eugenics, for example, used the limited concept of "intelligence" to justify genocide. I'm therefore sometimes troubled by the word "intelligence" in SETI. For one thing, we might not even be able to identify what intelligence is. And because of this, maybe we [will] someday make contact and [won't] even recognize that we've done so. But it's also important to think very critically about *why* we search for intelligence. Is there something special about intelligence? Does intelligence deserve more respect than whatever we might perceive to be nonintelligence? We might perceive microbes as nonintelligent life, for example. Does that life have a right to exist without us bothering it? Or is it just germs—just bugs that we are going to just bring back and study and pick apart?

We may not be able to recognize intelligence when we see it, and we may not respect or honor things we don't perceive to be intelligent. That is what we did in many colonial interactions. Certain countries in Europe made "first contact" with Indigenous peoples, perceived them to be nonintelligent and therefore not worthy of life, not worthy of respect or dignity. And that is troubling to me. What's going to be different next time?

Garzón: Agreed. But what would be a solution, then? Just using different terminology seems insufficient.

Charbonneau: Right. I've talked to a lot of scientists about examining the colonial legacy at play in SETI, and I'm sometimes met with resistance. I'm told, "You can't just cut words out of the dictionary" or "Obviously microbes on Mars are not the same as Indigenous people, and you can't offend a germ." All of which is, of course, probably true. But I think we would be foolish to not think carefully when we project our troubled concepts of intelligence and civilization onto the universe. It's not necessarily as ephemeral as you might think. SETI scientist Jason Wright once wrote, "Even more than thinking like an alien, we need to be sure we are able to identify what it means to think like a *human*." Decolonization may not be a metaphor, but metaphors and symbolism are big parts of human thinking.

People in general get frustrated when they hear statements such as "concepts of civilization and intelligence are socially constructed." It seems confusing and puzzling. It makes it seem like things aren't real. But actually it's the inverse. Words and socially constructed things are real because we are a verbal, social species. Things that are socially created still have a real-world impact; they're not imaginary. So when it comes to "decolonizing SETI," the metaphors do matter too. Maybe not to aliens, but to people on Earth. Being mindful of the histories and language we're invoking is the bare minimum of what we can do. And this is why including Indigenous voices is so critical. As Indigenous Studies scholar Sonya Atalay told the SETI project Breakthrough Listen, "Intent ≠ impact, we must consider both." It is not enough to just want to contact aliens and hope interaction will be friendly; we must critically examine our own history and words and stop assuming our good intentions will not result in harm. "Columbus" metaphors might not hurt an alien, but using them will hurt people on Earth.

Garzón: Let me push back on one aspect here, though. Might there be a degree of incompatibility between openness to other ways of being and SETI's core tenets? After all, SETI—all of astronomy, really—is built on the assumption of universality, that the laws of physics are the same throughout the observable universe regardless of one's social constructs. A radio telescope, for instance, will work the same way whether it's here on Earth or somewhere on the other side of the cosmos. Regardless of context, certain shared fundamentals exist to allow common, predictable, understandable outcomes. SETI takes this conceit even further by elevating mathematics as a universal language that can be understood and translated anywhere and by anyone. What are your thoughts on this?

Charbonneau: So let me preface this by saying I am not a mathematician. But I do write about math. And there are many anthropologists who study mathematical systems in different cultures. They see that, even on Earth, among human cultures, there are different ways of thinking about math. And while mathematics is the language we use on Earth in our hegemonic culture to describe what we are seeing, we don't know that another species will use that same language to describe what they are seeing. So while I don't want to discount universality, I do think any assumptions about this are perhaps optimistic, to put it kindly. The core of what I'm trying to say is that we must critically interrogate our assumptions about life and universality, because we will all too often find that they say more about *us* than aliens.

Garzón: Appreciating that some things can be too complex for universality to capture seems like a wise way to approach any human endeavor. You're saying there's never just one solution or one model that will be optimal for any given situation—multiplicity and plurality is as valid of a concept as universality, right? That seems to echo what you said earlier about listening.

Charbonneau: Yes, I think one of the best arguments for making SETI more diverse and for including diverse sets of thinkers is that the worst-case outcome from incorporating those other perspectives would just be the expansion of our pool of what civilizations might look like. There's really no downside. Not only are we being inclusive and trying to distance ourselves from historically oppressive behaviors—which I think is worth doing on its own—but we also may benefit SETI and other sciences because we can't be hurt by expanding our ideas of what a civilization or culture might look like. It just makes sense—if you want to listen to, and understand, alien cultures, you might as well start with your own species and planet first.

About the Author

Camilo Garzón is a writer, editor, reporter, freelance journalist, and multimedia producer and is currently working as a web producer for Scientific American. *Follow him on X (formerly Twitter) @camiloagarzonc.*

Life Is Complicated—Literally, Astrobiologists Say

By Natalie Elliot

T he hunt for extraterrestrial life has always been bedeviled by false positives—those occasions where scientists think they've found life but turn out to lack a wholly convincing case.

The archetypal example comes from NASA's twin Viking landers, which delivered controversial evidence of life on Mars in the mid-1970s. That evidence was a whiff of radioactive carbon wafting from Martian soil, hinting at microbial metabolism taking place within—but three other life-detection experiments each lander carried only found null results. More muddled data about life on Mars arrived in 1996, when scientists discovered what could have been microbial microfossils inside a Martian meteorite found in Antarctica. But subsequent studies showed the putative microfossils could have easily been produced by several other entirely abiotic routes. Most recently, researchers studying the atmosphere of Venus claimed to see significant amounts of phosphine there—a gas that, on Earth, is chiefly made by microorganisms. Yet soon other scientists had cast doubt on the validity of those measurements, and had postulated the gas—if it was there at all—was from some strange-but-lifeless form of Venusian volcanism.

In each case, the pattern was the same: initial excitement, followed by subsequent skepticism, and eventual dismissal. Time and time again, it seems, astrobiologists are only finding alien signs of life—so-called biosignatures—that are frustratingly inconclusive. This is in large part because astrobiologists by necessity seek the simplest, most robust forms of life that appear possible in harsh otherworldly environments, and the chemicals and structures we often associate with such organisms on Earth can often be produced abiotically. And, of course, the chemistry of alien life might be entirely different from what we observe on our own planet. Is there a better way to look?

A new theory published in *Nature Communications* contends that there is. Called assembly theory, it turns away from the search for simple chemical biosignatures, instead embracing life's fundamental complexity. It is based on the idea that any form of biology anywhere in the universe will encode life's information in complex assemblages of molecules that are measurably distinct from lifeless matter.

For study co-author Sara Walker, a biophysicist at Arizona State University, assembly theory is a landmark for the field, because it "presents the first complexity measure that is testable in the lab." More broadly, she says, it gives us "the first glimmer of our ability to connect deep theoretical ideas about the nature of life to empirical observables."

In astrobiology, appeals to complexity have been on the rise for a while now. In light of the ambiguous results that can come from research focused on simple chemical signatures, scientists have developed theories and definitions of life that look to more sophisticated processes—metabolism, adaptation, replication, evolution—that could help us distinguish living systems from nonliving ones. In 1994, for example, NASA adopted a complex definition of life: "Life is a self-sustaining chemical system capable of Darwinian evolution." The trouble is, the key concepts behind such advanced frameworks are themselves complicated, making them notoriously difficult to test and quantify. Ask, for instance, five different evolutionary biologists for their working definition of "Darwinian evolution," and you are likely to get five slightly different answers. As NASA's chief scientist, Jim Green, explains, "I can't build an instrument that is going to go out and find 'evolution,' 'reproduction,' or 'metabolism.'"

Assembly theory may offer a clearer, more general way to recognize life, whether familiar or alien. It builds on two related ideas: physical complexity and abundance, positing that as these two properties increase for any given object in any given environment, the chances of an abiotic origin decrease. Abundance tracks how often an object appears in an environment, whereas an object's complexity is measured by estimating the number of steps required for its assembly. Consider the difference between a seashore littered with water-worn pebbles—a situation that could easily be ascribed to a lifeless process—and one strewn instead with intricately sculpted seashells.

Although the theory is general and can pertain to many kinds of objects across a wide range of scales, the researchers looked at how it applies to molecules, arguably the most essential building blocks of biology that scientists can seek both in the lab and in space.

To rank molecular complexity, the team created a mass assembly index, which algorithmically assigns a mass assembly number (MA) to different kinds of molecules. As a proof of concept, they used this approach to index and rank 2.5 million molecules in a widely used chemistry database. A molecule with an MA of 1 has low complexity and thus a higher chance of abiotic origins; more complex molecules are assigned higher numbers. Composed of one atom of phosphorus and three atoms of hydrogen, phosphine gas—the putative Venusian biosignature—only merits an MA of 1. In contrast, the amino acid tryptophan earns an MA of 12 thanks to its elaborate structure of 11 carbon atoms, 12 of hydrogen, and a pair apiece of nitrogen and oxygen.

According to Lee Cronin, a chemist at the University of Glasgow who led the research, this exercise revealed that at a certain threshold—circa MA 15—a molecule's probability of abiotic production in Earth-like conditions becomes astronomically low. Less than one in about 600 sextillion, in fact, Cronin says. Thus, molecules ranking at an MA of 15 or higher should almost always be made by life.

So, does that mean that MA 15 is the surefire marker for life everywhere? No. For one thing, many low-ranking molecules can be biosignatures—such as the structurally simple molecular oxygen emitted into Earth's atmosphere by photosynthetic organisms. This means that, although it may decrease the chances of false positives in the search for life, assembly theory also correspondingly raises the likelihood of "false negatives" allowing genuine biosignatures to slip through investigative cracks. More broadly, Cronin says, although MA 15 seems to be the threshold value for life on Earth, the threshold could fall elsewhere for wildly different planetary environments. The trick, Cronin argues, is to use assembly theory to map the gap that must exist between the chemical combinations produced abiotically and those produced by living systems—here or anywhere else.

To further validate their approach, Cronin and colleagues double-checked their theoretical calculations of complexity by using mass spectrometry fragmentation to study a large sample of ranked molecules and substances, breaking each down into its constituent parts to confirm the number of chemical steps required to reassemble them. Those experimental results hewed closely to theoretical predictions, and reliably distinguished between a broad range of living, nonliving, and dead substances, including E. coli bacteria, yeast cells, plant alkaloids, ashes, coal, granite, limestone, and even beer.

One of the most exciting validations came courtesy of Cronin's collaborator and study co-author Heather Graham, an astrobiologist at NASA's Goddard Space Flight Center in Greenbelt, Md. To conduct a test of the theory, Graham's lab sent a set of blind samples. One of these was preserved biological material from a multimillion-year-old fossil. Another was a sample from the Murchison meteorite, a bolide rich in organic (but abiotic) carbon compounds that fell to Earth in 1969. Cronin's testing flagged the Murchison material as notable for its wealth of complex molecules, but still ranked it as below the threshold of MA 15 and thus lifeless. The fossil material, however, was identified as a signature of life.

For study co-author and NASA astrobiology postdoctoral fellow Cole Mathis, there was a striking moment at this stage of the research when a significant distinction became clear to all involved: the distinction between "a complex sample and a complex molecule." While a strange variety of chemicals like those present in Murchison might lead one to think that something like life was present there, it is actually the complex molecule, which indicates the organization of chemistry, that seems to be key to life.

The success of these results, and the publication of the work, brought out initial excitement. Steven Benner, a chemist at the Foundation for Applied Molecular Evolution in Alachua, Fla., who was not part of the research, says he and his colleagues are "extremely enthusiastic" about assembly theory. Even so, he adds, Cronin and colleagues still must address many unanswered questions about their work, especially whether it could actually be applied in "truly exotic environments." Benner has challenged Cronin to test the approach on samples of "semi-complex" material that Benner's group has synthesized from simple carbon precursors in lab conditions mimicking the atmosphere of Venus. "This is a real environment," Benner says, "one soon to be visited in a space mission again. If Venusian life exists in the clouds above Venus, it would need to follow a chemical logic very much different from the logic that is followed by life on Earth." This, Benner says, arguably makes Venus the best site for a near-term test of the molecular-complexity metric.

In response, Cronin has remarked that Benner's samples pose a particular challenge, as they are immersed in sulfuric acid—which decomposes organic molecules and thus lowers their detectable organic complexity. Nevertheless, Cronin says, "we are working on a way to reconstruct that complexity, so I remain hopeful that even in the most difficult samples, if the molecule is not broken, we can take a measurement."

In the meantime, Green and others at NASA have wondered whether assembly theory might be used to analyze data from the many mass spectrometers that have visited other worlds during the agency's various interplanetary missions. Green first considered the case of the mass spectrometer on the *Cassini* orbiter, which flew through and sampled plumes of water vapor venting from Saturn's icy moon Enceladus, but he realized that *Cassini*'s instrument only registered masses up to 100 atomic mass units (amu), and assembly theory only works for molecules weighing at least 150 amu.

Although they could reach 150 amu and beyond, instruments on the *Curiosity* and *Perseverance* Mars rovers fell short, too, lacking the specificity to study single molecular species for an MA measurement. Future missions, Green says, should all be equipped with mass spectrometers that register the higher mass and take measurements with greater specification. There is promise for NASA's *Dragonfly* mission, a nuclear-powered quadcopter slated to begin exploring the atmosphere and surface of Saturn's moon Titan in the mid-2030s. Graham points out that *Dragonfly*'s mass spectrometer, though it lacks some of the capabilities of lab spectrometers, will have the capacity to detect complex molecules.

In the future, other planned missions could seek out signs of life's molecular complexity at astrobiological hot spots across the solar system. Eventually, Cronin speculates, assembly theory might even be used to assess potential biosignatures remotely detected in the atmospheres of potentially habitable exoplanets by large telescopes.

For now, however, the approach has given theorists and experimentalists alike a wealth of new ideas for understanding—and seeing—life's cosmic complexity.

About the Author

Natalie Elliot is a science writer who writes about the origin of life, astrobiology, and the history of science. She teaches classics and history of science at St. John's College. Her work has appeared in Aeon *and* The New Atlantis.

Let's Search for Alien Probes, Not Just Alien Signals

By Avi Loeb

On blind dates, we search for others that resemble us, at least at some level. This is true in our personal life but even more so on the galactic dating scene, where we have been seeking a companion civilization for a while without success. While developing our own radio and laser communication over the past seven decades, the search for extraterrestrial intelligence (SETI) focused on radio or laser signals from outer space—two kinds of electromagnetic "messenger" that astronomers use to study the cosmos.

Over the same period, we have been also launching probes, like *Voyager 1* and *2*, *Pioneer 10* and *11*, and the *New Horizons* spacecraft, towards interstellar space. These could eventually reach alien civilizations, passively announcing our existence. But in 1960, at the dawn of the space age, Ronald Bracewell noted in a *Nature* paper that a physical space probe could also search for technological civilizations across interstellar distances. SETI should therefore explore this technique as well—a timely notion in the era of multimessenger astronomy, ushered most recently by the detection of gravitational waves.

This sort of exploration obviously could work both ways. Thanks to data collected by the Kepler space telescope, we now know that about half of all sunlike stars host a rocky Earth-size planet in their habitable zone. Within this zone, the planet's surface temperature can support liquid water and the chemistry of life. The famous Drake equation quantifies (with large uncertainties) the likelihood of receiving a radio signal from another civilization in our Milky Way galaxy. But it does not apply to physical probes that might arrive at our doorstep. The distinction resembles the difference between a cell phone conversation at the speed of light and the exchange of letters through surface mail.

It also suggests an addendum to the Drake equation: the number of probes in a volume of interstellar space can be expressed as the number of stars times the average number of probes produced per star, N. The nearest star system, Alpha Centauri, contains a close pair of sunlike stars (A and B) bound to a more distant dwarf star (C). This triple star system is about four light years away—but the nearest probe could be much closer—at a distance that is smaller by a factor of $(3N)^{1/3}$. In fact, this probe would be within the Earth-sun separation if civilizations produce on average a quadrillion ($N \sim 10^{15}$) probes per star over their lifetime.

If each probe weighs a gram, similar to what has been proposed by the Breakthrough Starshot initiative, then the total mass of a quadrillion probes would be comparable to the weight of a kilometer-size asteroid—completely negligible in the planetary mass budget. Such a meteor strikes the Earth every half a million years, and its size is smaller by a factor of several tens than the Chicxulub K/Pg impactor that killed the dinosaurs about 66 million years ago. Clearly, the actual number of interstellar probes would depend on the abundance and lifetime of technological civilizations per star, as well as the weight of each probe and the sophistication of its production technology.

My forthcoming book, titled *Extraterrestrial*, tells the story of the discovery of `Oumuamua, meaning "scout" in the Hawaiian language, by the Pan-STARRS facility in Hawaii on October 2017. As the first interstellar object detected near Earth from outside the solar system, it looked weird, unlike any comet or asteroid seen before within the solar system. The book details the unusual properties of `Oumuamua: it had a flattened shape with extreme proportions—never seen before among comets or asteroids, as well as an unusual initial velocity and a shiny appearance. It also lacked a cometary tail, but nevertheless exhibited a push away from the sun in excess of the solar gravitational force.

As a regular comet, `Oumuamua would have had to lose about a tenth of its mass in order to experience the excess push by the rocket effect. Instead, `Oumuamua showed no carbon-based molecules along its trail, nor jitter or change in its spin period—as expected from cometary jets. The excess force could be explained if `Oumuamua was pushed by the pressure of sunlight; that is, if it is an artificially-made lightsail—a thin relic of the promising technology for space exploration that was proposed as early as 1924 by Friedrich Zander and is currently being developed by our civilization. This possibility would imply that `Oumuamua could be a message in a bottle.

In September 2020, another unusual "asteroid" was discovered by-Pan STARRS, showing an excess push by sunlight without a cometary tail. This object, labeled by the astronomical name 2020 SO, was not unbound like `Oumuamua but instead on an Earthlike orbit around the sun. After integrating its orbit back in time, it was found that 2020 SO is a stray rocket booster, left over from a crash of the Surveyor 2 lunar lander on the surface of the moon in 1966.

Nevertheless, its discovery lends credibility to the notion that thin artificial objects with a large surface-to-mass ratio can be distinguished from natural objects based on their excess push away from the sun without a cometary tail. There is no way that `Oumuamua could have originated from our planet based on its high local speed, its large size and the inclination of its trajectory. Another way to put it is that `Oumuamua spent a fraction of a year within the orbit of Earth around the sun, and we know of no human-made object that was propelled to its trajectory over the year preceding its discovery.

When taking a vacation near a beach, I enjoy studying natural seashells, but on rare occasions I encounter an artificially made plastic bottle. Similarly, astronomers regularly spot naturally made rocks when monitoring comets or asteroids from the solar system, but perhaps `Oumuamua represents our first encounter with a plastic bottle, manufactured by an advanced technological civilization. Lightsails can be designed to weigh a gram per tens of meters squared of surface area, comparable to the area of `Oumuamua.

Interstellar probes could also maneuver to preferred trajectories that are not drawn from a random distribution. In particular, it is beneficial to bring them to rest relative to the star they intend to probe. In that case, the gravitational attraction by the star will pull them straight towards it. The focusing of their trajectories will enhance their density in the vicinity of the star, allowing more of them to travel through the habitable zone and spy for any technological signatures there. In the outer envelope of the solar system, such slow-moving probes would be hidden among the numerous icy rocks of the Oort cloud, that are loosely bound to the sun halfway to Alpha Centauri.

If the senders of the probes prefer to remain anonymous, they might choose to deposit them in the galactic parking lot, the so-called local standard of rest, which averages over the random motions of all stars in the vicinity of the sun. In this neutral frame of reference, it is not possible to identify where they came from. Surprisingly, `Oumuamua started in that frame before entering the solar system.

The data we gathered on `Oumuamua are incomplete. To learn more, we must continue to monitor the sky for similar objects. The realization that we are not alone will have dramatic implications for our goals on Earth and our aspirations for space. When reading the news every morning, I cannot help but wonder whether we are "the sharpest cookies in the jar." Are there extraterrestrials smarter than us in the Milky Way? The only way to find out is by surveying the sky for the multitude of messengers that they might be using.

About the Author

Avi Loeb is former chair (2011-2020) of the astronomy department at Harvard University, founding director of Harvard's Black Hole Initiative and director of the Institute for Theory and Computation at the Harvard-Smithsonian Center for Astrophysics. He also chairs the Board on Physics and Astronomy of the National Academies and the advisory board for the Breakthrough Starshot project, and is a member of President's Council of Advisors on Science and Technology. Loeb is the bestselling author of Extraterrestrial: The First Sign of Intelligent Life Beyond Earth *(Houghton Mifflin Harcourt).*

GLOSSARY

abiogenesis The theory that life originated from inorganic matter.

anomalous Deviating from what is expected.

anthropomorphic Human form or human qualities.

biosignature Signs of life.

biosphere The place where life can exist.

bitmap Binary data representing a digital image.

chemical fractionation The separation of chemicals during a transition.

Dyson structure Hypothetically, a large structure that can harness energy from a star.

ejecta Material thrown out from a larger item such as a volcano or a celestial body.

ephemeral Describing something that lasts a short time.

exoplanet A planet that orbits a star other than our sun.

hydrothermal Relating to hot water.

interstellar Something located in the Milky Way galaxy.

ionospheric Relating to the region in the atmosphere of a planet where charged particles are located.

laser spectroscopy Using a laser beam to analyze matter.

neutron star A dense celestial body that forms from the collapse of a larger star.

pseudoscience Theories and methods that are falsely claimed to be scientific.

sextillion A number followed by 21 zeros.

syntax The way words and language are structured.

FURTHER INFORMATION

"NASA Unveils Design for Message Heading to Jupiter's Moon Europa," Jet Propulsion Laboratory, https://www.jpl.nasa.gov/news/nasa-unveils-design-for-message-heading-to-jupiters-moon-europa.

"Report on the Historical Record of U.S. Government Involvement with Unidentified Anomalous Phenomena (UAP)," U.S. Department of Defense All-Domain Anomaly Resolution Office, https://media.defense.gov/2024/Mar/08/2003409233/-1/-1/0/DOPSR-CLEARED-508-COMPLIANT-HRRV1-08-MAR-2024-FINAL.PDF.

Ball, Philip. "The Final Ethical Frontier," *Aeon*, https://aeon.co/essays/as-space-gets-more-commercial-how-can-it-be-governed-ethically.

Derrick, Reilly, and Howard Isaacson. "The Breakthrough Listen Search for Intelligent Life: Nearby Stars' Close Encounters with the Brightest Earth Transmissions," The Astronomical Society of the Pacific, March 20, 2023, https://iopscience.iop.org/article/10.1088/1538-3873/acc1a1.

Kelvey, Jon. "How Scientists Decide if They've Actually Found Signals of Alien Life," *Popular Science*, https://www.popsci.com/science/extraterrestrial-life-seti-protocols/.

Kipping, David. "An Objective Bayseian Analysis of Life's Early Start and Our Late Arrival," *Proceedings of the National Academy of Sciences*, May 18, 2020, https://www.pnas.org/doi/10.1073/pnas.1921655117.

Kuthunar, Sharmila. "Low Oxygen May Smother Life's Prospects on Europa, Jupiter's Ocean Moon," *Scientific American*, March 4, 2024, https://www.scientificamerican.com/article/europa-jupiters-ocean-moon-may-lack-oxygen-for-life/.

Puranen, Emma Johanna, Emily Finer, Christiane Helling, and
    V. Anne Smith. "Science Fiction Media Representations
    of Exoplanets: Portrayals of Changing Astronomical
    Discoveries." Journal of Science Communication,
    March 4, 2024, https://jcom.sissa.it/article/pubid/
    JCOM_2301_2024_A04/

CITATIONS

1.1 New Evidence Discovered That Saturn's Moon Could Support Life by Ling Xin (December 14, 2023); 1.2 Life on Mars May Have Been Its Own Worst Enemy by Allison Gasparini (October 28, 2022); 1.3 At Jupiter, JUICE and Clipper Will Work Together in Hunt for Life by Jonathan O'Callaghan (February 16, 2023); 1.4 Mars Rovers Might Miss Signs of Alien Life, Study Suggests by Derek Smith (April 17, 2023); 1.5 NASA's Perseverance Rover May Already Have Evidence of Ancient Martian Life by Jonathan O'Callaghan (April 5, 2023); 1.6 Martian Crust Could Sustain Life through Radiation by Nikk Ogasa (August 1, 2021); 2.1 Here's What I Learned as the U.S. Government's UFO Hunter by Sean Kirkpatrick (January 19, 2024); 2.2 UFO Research Is Only Harmed by Antigovernment Rhetoric by Marek N. Posard and Caitlin McCulloch (September 13, 2023); 2.3 How Wealthy UFO Fans Helped Fuel Fringe Beliefs by Keith Kloor (August 25, 2023); 2.4 Bad Data, Not Aliens, May Be Behind UFO Surge, NASA Team Says by Leonard David (June 9, 2023); 2.5 To Understand UAP, We Need Megapixel Imagery by Avi Loeb (August 2, 2021); 2.6 Chinese Spy Balloon Saga Shows UFOs Deserve Serious Investigations by Mick West (February 16, 2023); 3.1 Can You Decode an Alien Message? by Shi En Kim (August 3, 2023); 3.2 Is E.T. Eavesdropping on Our Phone Calls? by Phil Plait (May 23, 2023); 3.3 Want to Talk to Aliens? Try Changing the Technological Channel Beyond Radio by Adam Mann (September 2, 2020); 3.4 Researchers Made a New Message for Extraterrestrials by Daniel Oberhaus (March 30, 2022); 3.5 Can "Conversations" with Whales Teach Us to Talk with Aliens? by Avery Schuyler Nunn (January 30, 2024); 3.6 When Will We Hear from Extraterrestrials? by Avi Loeb (August 15, 2021); 4.1 To Find Life in the Universe, Find the Computation by Caleb A. Scharf (June 22, 2023); 4.2 Most Aliens May Be Artificial Intelligence, Not Life as We Know It by Martin Rees and Mario Livio (June 1, 2023); 4.3 How Many Aliens Are in the Milky Way? Astronomers Turn to Statistics for Answers by Anil Ananthaswamy (July 16, 2020); 4.4 New Instrument Could Spy Signs of Alien Life in Glowing Rocks by Allison Gasparini (July 27, 2022); 4.5 JWST Heralds a New Dawn for Exoplanet Science by Jonathan O'Callaghan (January 23, 2023); 5.1 The Search for Extraterrestrial Life as We Don't Know It by Sarah Scoles (February 1, 2023); 5.2 How to Search for Life as We Don't Know It by Avi Loeb (September 26, 2021); 5.3 Cultural Bias Distorts the Search for Alien Life by Camilo Garzón (August 10, 2022); 5.4 Life Is Complicated—Literally, Astrobiologists Say by Natalie Elliot (November 23, 2021); 5.5 Let's Search for Alien Probes, Not Just Alien Signals by Avi Loeb (December 22, 2020).

Each author biography was accurate at the time the article was originally published.

INDEX